RESURRECT & RECLAIM

The True You

Martin Whelan
2019

GRATITUDE

Big love and a Massive Thank you to:

Tony Bostrom for his design, compilation, massive time and patience,

Helen 'Dancing Queen' Harvey for her ability to edit reason from my ramblings,

Everyone who knowingly, or unknowingly contributed to the content of this book

Introduction

Through reflection, through taking that *Bird's Eye View*; the breakdown of my marriage was a massive step towards my evolution. The *universe* must have felt the timing was right; I know now it *only gives us the challenge when the time is correct.* Perhaps I was *ready for it,* though at the time I felt like a child thrust onto a neon lit stage to perform without any script, without any rehearsal, and without a safety net to catch me if I fell!

The greatest step of my evolution came from one of the most traumatic things to happen to me, and there have been quite a few I can assure you! I was thrown against that *Wall*, a *Wall* designed to make me deal with and solve so many issues I had carried for years.

Upon this *Wall*, my future would be imprinted deeply. I could stand, or I could fall, it was totally my choice. Only now, through reflection, can I see that this event was my blessing; my defining time, my greatest opportunity to release the person I always wanted to be, and become the *Master of my own self.*

Martin Whelan

Contents

Foreword

Walking down a country road with the air around my face
The beauty of life surrounds me holds me deep in its embrace
Those things I never saw before when my mind made me live so unaware
A distance held me separate to a world without compare
Struggles that seemed so hard to face are now so simple to replace
When I open my eyes and contemplate the beauty of life served daily to my plate
Why did I not see it before why have I lived so long like a bore
Why did I have to wait for such pain to arrive to unlock the gate of life
I have never looked back a forward view was my track
But sometimes a moment to look back can check the rightness of the track
Following the herd even though deep down I knew it was absurd
Seemed the right thing to do make a life like others do
Just how lucky am I to have this chance to reply
To the calling inside that said my life's path was unwise
Unwise for just me no one else could know or perceive
What my heart said inside what I knew from a child
My challenge is now to stay true to my guide to be led from inside to live a life true and wise
To feel with every step that my life's purpose is met
To know I've lived like a child so free so wild

The word 'Resurrect' is conventionally associated to biblical terms. However, the definition for my use of the word 'Resurrect' is encapsulated within the definition *'the act of causing something that had ended or been forgotten or lost to exist again, to be used again'*.

Many of us, perhaps the majority of us, have become lost along the way. We have become diverted to such a degree that everything we inherently desired for this lifetime has become lost to the wilderness. I believe that armed with the focus of your desires, with a set of 'tools' and a process to follow, *this lost can become once again found*.

So how do I encourage you to work through this book, rediscover who you truly are and claim this magnificent Prize? What can I say to make you decide that this book will not be another paperback that sits on your self-help shelf with only the first 10 pages ever read? I must warn you, if you are looking for a 'light' read, an easy fix, a nip and tuck, a comfortable ride, please spend your money on another tome. To *Resurrect & RECLAIM The True You* takes guts and dedication.

You may ask what gives me permission to write *Resurrect & RECLAIM The True You*, and propose what I suggest? The only answer I can give you is that this is the road I have walked. I had no idea when I set out that the changes I desired would encompass so many aspects of my life. I couldn't contemplate my chosen road would require such depth of soul searching, the taking of so much action, constant evaluation, re-evaluation and sacrifice. Has it been worth it? More than any words could describe; though for you I will try!

To discover the *man* I had always wanted to be. Have full responsibility for every aspect of my life. Be able to walk this earth with a loving heart and compassion for others. Identify and consequentially experience several of my intrinsic desires for this lifetime. Negotiate myself through the daily pleasures and pains of *living a life* whilst seeing them all as one continuum. Yes, you bet it's been worth it!

I am no one special. My origins are from what some might describe as *the general populous*. This book is a guide dedicated to those of us who may consider ourselves *mainstream, one of the masses*, the *bulk of the population*; one of those people who *sit below the radar*.

The reason often given to our perceived profile is essentially determined to be the social environment within which we have found or find ourselves. This social environment appears to say *"look, its' OK for those others to seek happiness, find fulfilment and be spiritually free, but that's for them, it's for those who come from a more privileged situation than me"*.

It can appear that when we look at the icons of *freedom* there is a link to privilege, especially where money is concerned. Buddha was the son of a king. Yes, he gave it all up in search of his truth, but his underpinnings were within an environment where his focus was not on a daily need to put food on the table or a roof over his head.

People like Richard Branson are often viewed as being happy, as being free, as being able to follow their purpose in life. Through his endeavours he has achieved much and made many millions, but again his background was not one of lacking. His mother constantly challenged him; she goaded him that he was not *taking enough risk*!

Yet, how many of us have had this type of stimulus, this form of underpinning? *Just be careful, don't go too far. Remember; you need to eat! What if it doesn't work out? Who do you think you are! You must be mad! Don't come crying to me when it all goes wrong!* Are these perhaps more apt statements to describe the encouragement we have heard in our lives?

Those around us often mean well, but they have no concept as to the power of their messages. These emotionally loaded, fear-based messages, massively restrict our progress in life. They nullify our capacity, our objectivity and our clarity of vision to live the life we were meant to lead.

These powerful messages are like invisible hands that strive to pull our legs down in the swimming pool of life. Just as we start to get to grips with this *swimming* thing, as we start to move forward, those *hands of care* tug at us, they sap our confidence and pull our heads under the water. Little by little we move further and further away from the horizon we were meant to find.

Statistics say that 1% of the world's population controls 99% of the world's wealth. This may be so from a financial perspective but contemplate that there are over 7 billion humans on our planet earth. If we could *unearth* true happiness, the true wealth of life, for just 1% of the remaining 99%, we would gain the positive effects of 69.3 million humans finding their truth. Unlike money, however, your inherent truth cannot be taken away from you. You own it and once discovered, or more aptly, re-discovered, it is yours forever!

Yet how many people *truly* want to find this level of contentment, peace and happiness? How many people are willing to put in the work to release their enlightenment, their truth that is theirs alone? How many are prepared to find *their way*, a way that is not someone else's prescribed diet for a life to be lead?

When we take someone else's prescription, we begin to live a lie. Our body will tell us it's a lie. If we are courageous enough to listen, our body will tell us what to eat, what to drink, what is right, what is wrong but, to a massive degree, we have lost the art of *listening to ourselves*. We have lost the ability to listen to our own self prescription. We have lost the confidence to listen to our own inner voice. Our inner voice will guide us, nurture us, protect us and teach us how to find our own way home. Unfortunately, we have been conditioned in many ways to stop this form of listening.

We have been conditioned to believe what others say. We have been fooled that they know far more than us. We have been distracted into believing that they are far more intelligent, more learned, more knowing. But really, I ask you, how can this be? They are not and never can be *you*. No one on earth can know *you* as you do, or, perhaps more pertinently, as you used to!

The desire to transform our current world is often taken when we experience an acute level of pain. We literally *hit the wall*. We have listened to and tasted many quick fix potions and solutions. We have tried many *diets, disciplines, pills and instructions*, though nothing yet has quenched our thirst.

However, I say to you, this situation is all good; because now you are ready!

Everything you have faced to this point; the challenges, despair, trials, emotional pain and turmoil, have been your preparation ground to help you reach this point. You could not be here without going there, if you see my meaning.

Joy awaits the seeker when you realised how far you have strayed from your *Original True Self*, and then decide to take the necessary steps to realign yourself with who you truly are. These steps will leave you feeling fresh and alive. Your energy will vibrate, your eyes will glow; your heart will race towards the life you truly deserve to live.

The process *to Resurrect & RECLAIM the True You and find your Prize is no quick fix*. The process does not tell you what you should be at the end. The process is designed to *remove what 'is not you'* and create the space to release *the 'you', who you truly are*. Transforming our learnt and habitual behaviours takes time, effort and energy, however through these endeavours you will find your lifelong truth that you then own forever.

You must burn your past, your debilitating past. You must learn from, and then reduce to ashes, those long held Limiting Beliefs that ensnare you into submission on a daily basis. You need the courage to not know where you are going, and to often ignore what the outside world says. You eminently must be courageous enough to take full and total responsibility for your life and to live this life; the life you were meant to live before you were taken on a different road.

With this degree of courage, determination and a helping guide, you can find the peace, contentment and happiness of your own truth, a truth you will keep for lifetimes.

After each chapter I raise a set of questions for you to examine from your personal perspective. Your responses will begin to unearth amazing truths that will help you form specifics that you can work with later. Nothing you document will be right or wrong. The only judge of what you write will be you. You determine how deep and honest are the words you place on your paper.

 I have also highlighted a number of **Master Key** definitions that have surfaced for me as I have walked this path, describing either an understanding or a method to enable action to be taken.

Thank you for allowing me the opportunity to share what I have found. I truly hope *Resurrect & RECLAIM the True You* is a useful guide towards the *Prize* you have been seeking.

Martin

Chapter 1   *Realisations*

Looking through these eyes I feel a stranger, casting out on a world I just don't know

How is it I see no one before me, even though they're all that I have known

Surely it's just a misunderstanding, I know them but somehow I'm not so sure

Looking through a life of hope and hunger, looking through a life of choice and chore

Someday you will see it, someday you will know, that feeling in your body, a knowing that will show

Your truth, it lies before you, but you will never know 'till your eyes open to where your fear fears to go

The face now looking back from the mirror is the face you have wanted to see for, oh! so long. This face is authentic. No longer do you say, *"Who the hell is that?"* Now you say, *"Ah, there you are; where have you been?"*

You have earned your Prize. You have completed the necessary work to enable the universe to once again dance through your shoes. You have arrived back home to your authentic house. Now there is no more running. No more searching. No more feeling lost. You have found the Prize that inherently you always knew was there; although it had remained just out of reach of your fingertips for all this time.

Through your endeavours you have claimed your Prize. You have received your winners' medal and now can lavish yourself with pure gold. You have won, though this a different kind of winning. Unlike the momentary winning of a trophy, or of money, through the use of consciousness and awareness, you have rediscovered your *intrinsic Prize* that will continuously reward you for your lifetimes. You got lost, that was all. You got lost along the road like so many others, but now you are back.........but where had the *True You, that face now staring back from the mirror,* disappeared to?

 I would like you to imagine that you and your body resemble a house. This house, made of many bricks, has stood for a number of years. Once, your house was totally new, its doors fully open for adventure. Your house was fresh, alive and excited! Excited in anticipation of the experiences life would unveil before it. However, as the years passed, *a multitude of people and experiences visited this house of yours* and covered your walls with *their* words, *their* designs, *their* philosophies, *their* perspectives and *their* beliefs of how your life should be.

Wall of Self Esteem

Through the instructions of these *visitors*, your house no longer displayed your original descriptions. These original writings described your purest purposes, desires, inner principles and values for this lifetime.

It had been re-decorated and re-designed by *others* to portray how they wanted your house to look and be. At your birth the bricks of your house, your *Wall of Self Esteem*, had been clear, fresh and unpolluted, displaying only the *words* which described your natural talents and your inherent gifts. However, after these *visitors* had crossed your threshold, *your own* words had been completely covered by the writings of others.

At some point, be it six, sixteen, thirty-six, sixty-four, eighty-seven matters not; a minority of us begin to search for answers to questions that arise from the deepest depths of our being. We start to realise that the life we are living is not the one we were intended to live.

We begin to *consciously* realise the existence of these external writings, realisations that cause deep despair within the seeker. Massive questions surface that expose the distance between how we are currently living our life from the true, untarnished person we originally were, and were meant to be.

These internal questions begin to uncover how the *words* of others, together with the events and experiences we have experienced, have seeped so deeply into our skin. These questions reveal how these words and experiences now affect the way we operate *unconsciously* in our inner and outer worlds.

If you were to ask yourself the following questions, how would you 'truly' respond?

When you wake up in the morning how do you feel? Do you just want to turn over, pull those covers high, or do you jump out of bed to meet a fresh new day?

Do you hope that something good might happen today or do you know what your day will hold?

Do you have boundless energy, or do you yawn all day?

Do you drag yourself around or is there a spring in your step that others notice?

Can other people 'feel' you when you are around?

Does your energy pulse through your skin, or do you feel enclosed, captured within your form?

Do you feel your dreams? How close to them are you living?

How small are you living or are you walking tall?

What limitations do you believe are *reality* for you?

What fears stop you in your tracks? How disempowering are they?

How do they affect you being the true you?

How would it feel to not carry these fears with you each and every day?

In my experience, the majority of people will never in this life time ask themselves these type of questions, or, if these types of question do arise within them, they bury them again as quickly as they were unearthed.

For some of us however, that minority of which I speak, we reach a point where these questions refuse to be buried. They burn with the intensity of the sun during our waking moments. They are implicit in our dreams, and they refuse to accept our insistence to extinguish their raging flame.

We, *The Chosen Few*, hit a point where we have no option but to begin to reach, search and grope in the darkness for answers to our deepest questions. We begin to realise that we have lost ourselves in a world of suggestion, a world of mass information, which is constantly *selling us something* to direct us towards what is forecasted to bring happiness to our lives.

We are sold a formula where everything is possible. The dream life we crave is just ahead of our fingertips, as long as we keep on believing in *their* way. Just work harder and harder, push and push further, climb and climb higher until we achieve the goal.

We set off, following this prescribed formula. We push and push harder, reach and reach higher; climb and climb higher and reach the *top of that desires ladder*. Yet, when we make that top rung, when we *succeed*, when we get *there*, when we *achieve the goal*, many of us reach a point where what we have been sold feels somehow meaningless. Even by achieving the *goal*, even when we obtain those desired *things,* we are left feeling empty. We are left with no juice, no vivacity and no lasting, deep-felt happiness as we go through our day. We have received the *prize* for our endeavours, yet as we open the box and look inside, it feels like yet another empty promise.

Until we reach this crisis point of *Realisation*, we manage to somehow hold ourselves together. We deal with the challenges that come our way but then, at a point somewhere along the continuum of time, enough is enough. The proverbial dummy gets spat out of the mouth. We intuitively know we have had enough of ignoring this underlying feeling of dissatisfaction. At first we cannot understand what is going on. Turmoil reigns as we try to find answers to why these questions haunt us. All we do *know* is that our instincts and intuition are screaming at us to change the course of our life.

Our pragmatic, logical mind informs us that the life we have experienced to this point is *the reality of life*. We recall dreams we had along the way, but these dreams now lie covered under the rubble of our daily demands. The *educated* mind tries to convince us that this *Strive to achieve model* is the *right way*, it is *we* who are wrong; it is *us* who haven't adapted well enough to the model yet!

Furthermore, we begin to justify that the leading of *your own life* is only for the *chosen few*. Living your own way is for the lucky ones, the special ones, the gifted ones. Most certainly it is not available to people like *us* who have had the *journeys* we have travelled to this point! You recall your challenges. You relive your disappointments. You rationalise the reasons why the life you were meant to lead now seems so very far away. Yet still you dream!

These intrinsic dreams do not confine themselves to your sleeping hours. They appear before your eyes when you take time over lunch to be alone. These images sit with you on the bench in the park. These dreams probably bare no semblance of reason in relation to the life you currently are leading, or, quite literally, to where you are sitting. They appear to have no realistic feasibility of transforming into any sort of reality, especially from within your current circumstances, capabilities or financial situation.

The *dream* I am describing here mostly resembles a feeling. We all have day to day dreams. Dreams are our minds way of trying to complete something that remains unfulfilled, a situation for which we seek completion. Perhaps, however, we need to replace the word *dream* or even *feeling* with the phrase *the call of our inner nature*. Our inner nature, our inner communicator, speaks to us in a variety of ways. It is a *voice* that continually informs and guides us towards our individual core desires and destiny. This communicator *knows you better than you do!*

For you now, however, being one of the *Chosen Few,* this force, this inner communicator, has begun to speak powerfully again to you. It spoke to you as a child when you *unconsciously* knew what truly made your heart beat, before your *learning* commenced. For example, as a child you may have seen and felt yourself standing upon a stage, singing to a massive audience who screamed your name, they chanted for more, with tears of pure joy in their eyes as you moved their emotions.

Now, for some *unknown* reason, this inner force has started to talk to you, though now it is speaking with a ferocity you cannot ignore. It has brought you to a grinding halt. It has gripped your throat so tightly that you know you will die unless you begin to listen to this *natural* calling.

As one of the *Chosen Few*, you are very fortunate. You have been *asked* to stop and reconsider your direction. You have been chosen by your natural force to contemplate where you are within this lifetime and determine whether you are living the life you were meant to lead. You are being *asked* to look at yourself in that mirror and contemplate if you truly know the person staring back at you. You are being *asked* to look at your eternal, deepest, all-consuming desires and consider if they are being satisfied. You are being *asked* to reveal the creature that has always been within.

Once you have the courage to look inside, there is a very high possibility that you will discover just how far you are from your intended shore. The distress which surfaces for many of us through these realisations can literally begin to blow our mind. How could I possibly be living so incorrectly? How could I have betrayed myself for so long? How could I have been so stupid, so naive, so passive, so ignorant? I ask you now to be kind to yourself, as this is all good.

The Wall of Denial

 As crazy as it may seem, this point you have reached, the realisation as to the existence of *The Wall of Denial* is an incredible place to reach. The vast majority of people will move through this lifetime unaware that there might be another way. They will not hear, or certainly not listen to, their callings. They will remain within the *real world*, the *world of logic*, the *world of reason*.

To move forward we must realise this as a *fact*. We may well be surrounded by people and loved ones who will stay the way they are forever. Perhaps the world is not ready for us to all become aware. All I do know is this. We, *The Chosen Few*, are blessed to be asked to reveal our inner treasures and face our *Wall of Denial*.

At this point it needs also to be understood that the *realisations* you arrive at surrounding the way you want to live in the future, may not be seen as correct for *those* who want us to be and perform in a certain way, in a way we always have before.

 We have been **conditioned and schooled** with what is seen as the *correct* way to live. After our initial years, we must participate in a formally recognised education, seek to gain excellent qualifications, adhere to the rules of the land in which we live, be politically correct, be in accord with a religious doctrine, create financial security, get married with 2.4 children, have a personal policy to continually improve in measurement to our peers, and work incredibly hard and fast completing all these tasks!

This *conditioning*, this *correct* way, is designed to provide a template of the human being to enable us to negotiate living in *the world* today. This conditioning starts from the moment we are born. It is a process of instruction and learnt behaviours which teach us how to conform and perform to society's requirements. It is a set of instructions that are put in place by others, but it unfortunately often totally ignores our inner nature, our naturalness and our innate individuality.

I want to challenge you now. Sometimes we need to look at the widest edge of a polarity to get a perspective of the other position. We need to be exposed to an extreme view of the world that we perhaps have never ventured to investigate before we can decide upon how relevant this is to our personal perspective. Often, the middle ground is the correct path to take, however, unless we look at the full spectrum of ground we are to cover, how can we really know where that 'middle ground' is?

Imagine that the *True You* is a wall within that house of bricks that form your body. When you were born, words were written on each brick within this wall. Descriptions and definitions of the *True You* were inscribed on each brick and were totally clear for you to see. At this stage of life you were completely free, completely pure and totally secure in who and what you wanted to achieve in this lifetime.

These bricks are inscribed with your core purpose or purposes, your aspirations and your fundamental desires which your inner nature wishes you to fulfil. Written on these bricks are all the intrinsic elements that will create for you pure joy and happiness should you follow their inscribed messages. Your life's description is etched within these bricks as a map for you to follow.

At your core you may be a writer, gardener, pianist, banker, mathematician, cleaner, pilot, inventor, comedian, scientist, academic, hairdresser, electrician, painter, politician, dancer, nurse, singer, historian, botanist, the list is endless.

Outside of these core inscriptions you are completely clean. Nothing else is written on your *Wall of Self Esteem*. There is nothing to hinder your progress, your joy or your march towards your individual happiness. You are clean of beliefs, experiences and external influences. At this point, the fundamental components of your internal nature, your intrinsic desires, are as yet unblemished by anything or anyone outside of your true self.

Unfortunately, as human beings, we are incapable of independently growing and flourishing into our true selves. We cannot survive without the support and influence of others. As we are born, we become subject to these external forces. Parents, grandparents, carers, tutors, events and experiences gradually begin to write their own messages upon our pure *Wall of Self Esteem*. These new messages, posted upon our wall, are written from *their own* beliefs, *their own* experiences and *their own* conditioning and predeterminations.

These *external teachers* immediately begin to write *their own* definitions of how life should be for you, together with what you should, or should not be, allude to and desire. In essence, they begin to cover over and replace the pure inscriptions on your *Wall of Self Esteem* with the pen of *their own words*.

In most cases these *external teachers* are not knowingly being destructive to us. For example, as a parent we believe that we must show our children *the way* that will protect them and give them a framework for their own development and protection. We believe we need to provide a platform for the child's growth to enable them to make their own way in the world. Parents feel a duty to provide certain disciplines and guidance that enables their child to be acceptable within the requirements of society and make their way in the world of today.

However, where do these definitions of *societal acceptability* come from? Who determines the prescribed social norms? Who determines the expectations of society today and deems that this behaviour is right, this behaviour is wrong, this way is acceptable, this way is not?

Let's consider a young child, up to two-years old. At this age the child will not be aware of any societal norms or rules to adhere to. If they get bored, if they don't want to shop anymore, if they get hungry, if they want to be out of that buggy, you can bet that everyone within earshot is going to hear about it! The child will scream. They will kick. They will burn you with the raging anger in their eyes! They will become inconsolable, irrespective of whoever is in the vicinity! They will inform us in no uncertain way that this situation is against what their inner nature is telling them they want to be doing. The parent tries numerous methods to appease the situation. Food, distraction, promises, threats or any appeasing action is used to try to move the child into a behaviour that is acceptable to those around them.

Yet within another moment, there is a revolution. Suddenly, from nowhere, comes a total transformation. The child becomes blissfully happy. They have found their favourite toy. The total despair they felt moments earlier has disappeared completely. Their face is now full of joy. Their tears are no more; their body is totally relaxed and calm.

At this age the child can experience 100% of the extremities of their

Spectrum of Emotion

emotions. They feel massive highs and massive lows, within seconds of each other. At the top end they are blissfully happy, completely at one with all around. At the bottom end of the scale they feel deep despair, complete frustration and dejection, a total loss of self-control.

Little by little they are taught that this *way* of behaviour, this extreme shift on their emotional spectrum, is unacceptable. They are expected to conform to societal acceptability; otherwise they will not be accepted or *fit in*. They will be seen as an outcast, seen as the horse in the corral that could not be broken. They are effectively taught they must fit in if they want to survive.

When they start to behave in the way that is *acceptable* to society, they begin to experience reward and acceptance from others. Their behaviour is seen as in accord with expectations, and they are applauded for it. The world of suppression and self-denial has begun. Inadvertently, those that love and treasure the child the most have begun to replace their inner nature with *external* expectations.

As the child grows, they experience how the outside world impacts upon how they behave on a daily, hourly or minute-by-minute basis. People now look for *consistency* from them. They want to believe that they *know them,* their *little ways,* and *know* who they are and how they operate. They can relax and place the child in a compartment identified *known and acceptable.*

Even at this early stage, they have begun to learn that being their *True Self* is often not the way others and society wishes them to be. Many *Bricks* within their *Wall of Self Esteem* have been removed and re-inscribed with an *external* description of *the way*. No longer do they feel 100% of their emotional scale. Perhaps, even before the age of 5, they have been reduced to 70% of their natural, spontaneous self.

The child has begun to operate within a smaller dimension of their emotional spectrum scale. They still, however, feel the feelings. They explode from time-to-time but now, not so often. They still run but not quite as free, they dance, but now they have begun to look into *others'* eyes for acceptance. They jump, but not quite so high. Whose face do you now see in that mirror?

Usain Bolt, arguably the greatest short distance runner of all time, was taken to the doctor when he was a child. His family were worried about his huge degree of energy. He was always running and jumping, always full of power and activity. They asked the doctor if he would ever calm down and if he needed medication to curb his hyperactivity. The doctor informed the family "this boy is perfectly healthy, leave him be". How different might he; and the world be, if that doctor had reached a different conclusion!

Up to the age of five the child has mostly been *schooled* by parental guides. Now comes the time they enter another school; the school of formalised education! Once again, they become subject to *others'* rules and forces, though now the influence is different!

When the child enters formalised education there is a significant difference to comprehend. The curriculum, the rules and forces the child experiences now comes from people who are unknown to them. In general, to this point, they have been guided by people who are close to them, people who know something about who and what they are. Now the game has changed!

The world of formalised education is determined by people who do not know *us*. These are people within an establishment who allude to have our best interests at heart, yet they are people from an establishment who do not know us! They do not know what our unique aspirations are, they do not know what we truly want to achieve; they do not know what our individual strengths are.

When politicians proclaim that we need to *educate* people, what do they really mean? Are they truly looking to educate us as individuals, enable us to live the most blissful, enlightened life, based upon our unique aspirations?

Consider with me for a moment. Is the education provided designed to maximise our capabilities as a unique individual, or is it designed for us to become a worthwhile commodity in the market place? Is the education on offer matched to our individual capabilities and desires, or is it a generality? Is it a one size fits all suit which fits only Mr Average? Where are we as an individual in all this? Where is our interpretation, where is our flavour on the subject?

What happens when our *ability or style* of learning falls outside of society's educational norm? What happens when we do not agree with the *facts* that are being placed before us, *facts* which we are required to accept as present and correct? What happens when we have a reluctance to just accept what others say until it is our own personal experience?

In my experience, *challengers* of the *prescribed truth* are labelled trouble makers, renegade students, misfits, nonconformists. The challenger is detained until they do what they are told; the only way forward is to concede. We are made to feel incompetent and incapable of being educated. The challenger is often isolated from those who do *appear* to have the designated societal norm capability to *learn*.

We can begin to feel that we may never fit in. We start to fall into a classification of student who will only be capable of certain types of jobs. Immense pressure is applied from those in power who inform us that we had better start to conform, just accept what we are being told and get on with it!

Spectrum of Emotion

After all, they suggest, "it's just for a while. Just get those all-important examination results, invest just a few years at the most and then you can be free to do whatever you like. We think to ourselves "obey the rules for a while and then hey, as they say, I will soon be free to make my own decisions". But I want you to consider something. How long does it take to condition the human being?

Western formalised education is normal from the age of five to sixteen, and for many who enter university, into their early twenties. We are not talking days or weeks here, we are talking years! Studies inform us that if we do something for sixty days it becomes a habit, a habitual behaviour that becomes the way we automatically, unconsciously operate. What habits, then, will we form during four thousand and fifteen to five thousand and seventy-five days of *formalised education*?

How far will you be from what is *the truth* to you? How many bricks in your *Wall of Self Esteem* will now have been replaced? Where is that child who screamed so loud and free, that child who was determined to live as they wanted? What degree of the *Spectrum of Emotions* are we now capable of experiencing? Perhaps 30%, if we're lucky?

Spectrum of Emotion

So, the educational groundwork has been done. The child to adolescent has learnt some skills that have *value* in the marketplace. Now they enter the wider social world. The world of commerce, the world in which we earn our living and the world of further political influence and self-professed *leaders*!

As one of the majority, we will have a need to pay our way in life through the medium of exchange. We exchange our skills, time energy and endeavour in return for money, with the potential opportunity to experience all that the material world can offer.

This society, with its orientation to money, has been created by man. We need money to house ourselves, have clothes on our backs and money to exchange for the necessities of life. Often at this stage relationships form; bringing children and additional responsibilities which consume large quantities of time, focus and energy. We trade our learnt skills and marketable assets to satisfy the needs of the home and our all-encompassing responsibilities.

We reach a point where the vast majority of the bricks within our *Wall of Self Esteem* have writing all over them. Virtually all of our true self descriptions have been written over, have been almost erased, and replaced by the calls of society. Our time is consumed with ensuring we retain our livelihood and in the nurture and development of others. We have little time, energy or capacity to look at our own needs and our own place on this earth. We are totally distracted by external needs and responsibilities.

We smile through eyes that see a world of demand, work and effort, though often behind these eyes is an empty valley, which calls to us through a hushed voice during our times of quiet. Pressures abound to work longer for that raise or promotion, work ever harder, smarter and faster, in the never-ending pursuit of increased profit, efficiency and effectiveness. Our natural way of being has become a robotic existence.

Space for self-reflection, spontaneity, doing nothing, disappears. A perpetual feeling of being more on the hamster wheel than the hamster pervades. How did life become this? Who am I? Is this all there is? Am I free or just a slave? Is my smile real or just a social product? Is it a facade to convince others, and myself, that I'm OK? Can I do this? Am I making good progress? Do I know what I am doing?

In the main, we don't even know that we have been distracted. We are bombarded with messages. The media of politics, advertising, controversy, war, famine, banking collapse, soaring house prices, utility costs, have and have not's. Myriad, powerful messages, bludgeon us subconsciously into submission.

To cope with the vast quantity of messages sent through today's multi-source media channels, we must consciously decide which or any of these messages we respond or react to. Subliminally, we are constantly filtering this mass of messaging to cope with the volume. We have to desensitise ourselves to what is happening in the wider world for us to cope with our day. If we responded to all the triggers we receive during the course of just one day we would be in chaos, we would collapse, we would explode.

Some of us reach a stage where we begin to become acutely aware that, knowingly or unknowingly, others want to control us. They want us to be, do, say, act and respond in accordance with what they want from us. This *realisation* is so hard to comprehend that most people refuse to see the evidence in front of them. They *simply* run away or take further measures to distract themselves. They *bury* the evidence. It is mightily hard to comprehend that others could be so cunning, so devious, so manipulative, so uncaring. Years of *learning* together with *their inscribing* is now so deeply etched upon our *Wall of Self Esteem*, for most of the time we essentially have no idea as to what we are doing.

Don't think that this level of conditioning has happened to you? Just think of a *little phrase*, normally used at a specific time by someone close to you. Can it not induce within you massive feelings from your dark distant past? Just hearing those words, said with *that* tone, can change your breathing, your pulse rate, your physiology, your facial tension. These physical changes all induced through a simple phrase, delivered at a specific time and place.

These triggers can be used by *unconscious* people, often parents, brothers or sisters or people close to us, who are unaware of what they are unearthing through their communications. Their unawareness often brings about conflicts in discussions, *"what did I say?"* exclaimed just after a full-scale eruption has cascades from the wounded party!

Now, consider the possibility where people or organisations *are* aware of their objectives. Consider that the other party *knows* what they are doing. Consider that they are skilled in the art of control and manipulation.

Remember that this chapter is dedicated to Realisations. Until I started to *clean up my act* this type of question, or alternative view I am about to pose, seemed so far removed from who I had previously been. This type of question started to surface as I started to see the world and its inconsistencies in a completely different way, and I have to say, some things I became aware of just are not pretty!

There are over 7 billion people on this planet. 7 billion different worlds, 7 billion ways of seeing things, yet we are often asked to adhere to disciplines that may have been written thousands of years ago! Where is it written for instance that all anyone should want is to live a blissful life, and, as part of this bliss, you should construct *your own* disciplines by which you will live your life? You should construct *Your own* commandments you will live by, defined by *your own* intrinsic values. Commandments that you live in accord with, which relate specifically to how you want to show up in this world, a set of guidelines that fit totally with you?

You will never find this written by those who wish to control how you think, behave, act or work. They want us to operate in accordance with what *they want* from us. They would never formally write such a thing down, however, because, if you were *free to choose your day*, where would they be?

We might consider it impossible for humanity to function without government; yet the birds have no government! The fish in the sea have no government. The trees have no government. Left to their own devices, left as nature intended them to be, they flourish ungoverned.

The human being is supposed to be the most intelligent species on the planet, yet we are the only species who believe we need government, religion, police and military might to protect us. We need government, religion and law enforcement to show us how to behave, worship, respect, work, interact with other people and flourish. Creatures and things many consider far below in the hierarchy of life, do all these things naturally. We are *conditioned to believe* we need others to tell us how to do these things. Where truly are we in the hierarchy of life?

I *believe* that the vast majority of us want to live in harmony. Most people want to live in harmony with their surroundings, their families, their neighbours and their friends. People want to enjoy good food, excellent health, relaxation and relative comfort. Most of us do not naturally aspire to own yachts, planes, multiple houses, eat caviar, have diamonds, fame and fortune to allow us to demonstrate how glorious we are as creatures. A great life for most of us would consist of a natural smile on our face and a warm glow of contentment from an inner happiness of a life lived in harmony with all around.

Unfortunately, this will not satisfy those with a vested interest in our ability to *contribute*. The word *vested* is interesting. The dictionary describes it as *'having an unquestionable right to the possession of property or a privilege.'*

Living in harmony and in freedom is not popular with those who seek power, control and large quantities of money. It is a known fact that 1% of the worlds' population *control* the remaining 99%, especially where money is concerned. I believe we are influenced from birth to fit in, conform, obey, but most importantly; we are being *reconstructed* to become the type of worker and contributor *they* want us to be. When someone refuses to be twisted, organised, re-modelled and reshaped, in accord with the vested interested requirements, the consequences can be dangerous.

In 1968 Dr Martin Luther King was killed. A historical fact that has taken place within many of our lifetimes. In 1955 a person with black skin had to give up their seat on a bus for someone whose face was white! How advanced is that?

Dr King had a comprehension of how the 'world' can operate when he stated, *"I may not be with you when you reach the promise land"*. Prophetic words, yet just consider the bravery of the man for one moment. He knew there was every chance that he would be killed for saying his truth, yet he still stood proud, he still stood in front of the world and honoured his beliefs. He still maintained his *own Commandments* even when faced with the ultimate knowledge.

'OK's-ville'

Spectrum of Emotion

So many other examples of Denial and Influence are available when we begin to look. Banks can legally lend 9 times more than they are worth. Queen Victoria decreed she needed 5 wars a year to satisfy her empire. Britain made 12 million Chinese drug addicts to open up the tea trade with China. The USA is the only country to have dropped an atom bomb. Yet how do these countries promote and project themselves to the outside world? They portray themselves as the leaders of the free world, the peacekeepers; the countries to turn to in crisis! So much deception, so much distraction!

I said this piece would not be pretty! I said that it wouldn't be filled with nice fluffy stuff, though I hope you can see why I wanted to share just some alternative perspectives from the ones you may currently hold as true. If I have stimulated just one question that resonates within you, and you go and investigate it for yourself, then it will all have been worthwhile, for this is a key piece towards our growth.

The journey to enable you to *Resurrect & RECLAIM the True You* hopefully will not require you to face the ultimate challenge! However, it will require you to challenge your deepest held beliefs and your conditioning, your automatic reactions to stimulus which have been installed into you over many, many years.

These snippets of alternative information I found massively difficult to take on board, as they were directly opposed to anything I had believed before. Some might say *where have you been, I've known this for years,* but I had no clue. I believed in what I had been told and taught as one of the masses. I was naive to a fault, but I guess I also didn't want to believe that these types of things went on.

With all of the misinformation we receive, it is now completely understandable for me to understand why we can be so distracted, so effectively, from our core beliefs, desires and true purpose of life.

Through continuously being subjected to the conditioning of *outside forces,* our natural exuberance and responses are reduced ever further to a fraction of our origination. We now at this stage probably live at 5-10% of our potential power!

You have arrived in a world I call *Ok'sVille.* You look out at the world through a window the size of a *postage stamp.* Your panorama of what life truly is, and can be, has become miniscule. The dreams you had as a child, the wacky aroma of what your life's expectations were before the sands of time blocked your doors, are now seen as just childish escapism. You have been reduced to a belief system created by *others'* belief systems. You don't want to admit it, but you know this is right; otherwise you would not be here, searching for the reasons why.

As I have previously stated, I believe just a small number of us reach a point during where we have no alternative but to stop and review our total way of living. This small number will review if the life they are living is truly what it's all about. Why the band of us who go in search is so small I do not know. Perhaps it's because we are all at different stages of evolution, perhaps it's because if all of us took this time to review our life and our purpose, we would have chaos! No trains running, no bread baked, no schools open, hospitals closed, sewage systems inoperable, no gas for the cooker. We would be returned to nature, to the natural world; though perhaps that chaos would be real progress!

No, it is my belief that just a few of us reach this point, but that's really OK. This is correct, this is natures balance. Those of us who reach this point; call it luck, call it a curse, call it fortune or misfortune, destiny or unconscious desire, matters not. What truly matters is to hear its call. To not listen to ourselves, to not listen to our natures calling, is a *criminal denial* of our intrinsic home.

At previous points in your life you may well have had these same *callings*. Callings of discomfort, confusion, unease and a *knowing*; yet at those times you managed to quell their calling with distractions and activities that covered up the underlying suffocation you felt surrounding the life you were living. Now, no matter how hard you try to distract yourself, try to quell those emotions, try to divert your intrinsic nature, you remain incapable. Nature has thrown you against the *Wall of your Socialised Self* to ask you, to shout and scream at you, to review and conclude how closely you are living to who you truly are.

At first, through shaking hands that cover your eyes, you begin to look at the writings that are now upon your wall. You may well be distraught at what you find. You may be traumatised to find that you no longer know who you are, what you stand for or even how you feel. You may unveil a catalogue of disharmony, a chasm, a massive gap between the *True You* and the *You* that you have become.

You want to run, hide under the stairs, or just simply disappear. You feel traumatised by the lie you have been living. You want to replace the lid upon that box of delusion, a box you have again found but wish had never opened. You feel a flood of emotions that appear to have no rationality. Spectres dance in front of your eyes with a song of distant dreams, fears, longings and desires, that you buried long ago, deep from sight.

I implore to you that the box now opened is full of treasure. Like gold in a mine, the treasure is covered with layer upon layer of unwanted material, but it is there just the same. This is a treasure that, when it is unpacked, examined and explored, will enable you to discover a life of joy unimagined.

Total Responsibility

 Your challenge now is to take the Master Key of *Total Responsibility*. Only you as an individual can decide if your desire is strong enough to expose, understand and choose to follow your original writings. You must remove those layers of dust, dirt, hard core and concrete which have collated and formed over the years. These layers have distanced you from your unique manuscript. You alone must decide if you are prepared to do whatever it takes to live your life. I believe that life's true meaning is to strive to experience your individual, core desires and aspirations that were written within you at your birth.

You were not meant to live to the writings inscribed by others. Only by living *your own story*, the life that life intended for you, can life bring you fulfilment, joy, pleasure, happiness, growth and your ultimate completion.

Realisations

Personal Review

- What degree of *conditioning* do you feel you have experienced?

- Can you identify the major areas of *conditioning* you have experienced? What do you feel has been the impact upon your **Wall of Self Esteem** through this *conditioning* on your life so far? How much has it restricted you?

- To what degree on your *Spectrum of Emotion* do you believe you feel? 80% 60% 20% 5%? What are you judging this against? Are you living in *OK'sVille*?

- The emotions you currently feel, are they positive or negative, happy or angry?

- What do you currently do that takes you to your highest level on the *Spectrum of Emotion*? What takes you to the bottom?

- How far away do you feel from the *True You*? Again, how are you measuring this? Do you feel you have hit the Master Key - **Wall of Denial?** How does it feel? What has brought you here?

- What is your *world view*? How wide is the way you look at what is going on out there? Are you living in a *postage stamp world*?

- What did you used to believe but over time this belief changed? *What* and *Why* did it change?

- How much of the Master Key - **Total Responsibility** do you truly take for your life?

Remember, this is all good. You are here for a reason.

You have the potential to live the life you were born to lead.

Chapter 2   *Experiences*

Ha! Ha! World you've got me now, I guess you must have been looking for another clown

A tumbling act of such magnitude, the crowds will shout 'we've never seen such a fool'

You're looking for what, ha! Ha! You know what, you would have more luck being a despot

An average man sets out with a plan, a plan to re-define and walk a different line

What is happiness? What is it to be happy? How would you know if you were happy, truly, lastingly happy?

My definition of true happiness is when you feel and *know* deep inside that you are living in complete accord with your intrinsic nature, your spirit and your core desires. When there is a flow to your life, elegance surrounds you. You reach a point where you *know* you have *arrived* and are living the way you were always meant to live.

This *knowing* emanates from deep inside. Whatever it is, it just *feels right*. There are no questions that surround its conclusion. This *knowing* is instinctual, intuitive, soft and pure.

The further we are away from this accord, the lower the level of our personal happiness. Personal happiness is selfish. Selfish in the term that no-one else on earth can *know* what *our* true happiness is.

The conditioning and experiences we encounter along the way, together with our retained remembrances and related emotions, have life long, dramatic impacts upon the degree of happiness we feel.

Without fully understanding what *true happiness* means to us, we begin to live in that place I call *OK'sVille*. Over time, we feel that the range of our *Emotional Spectrum* becomes miniscule. Over time we learn to be respectful, unobtrusive, calm, non-confrontational, disciplined, all to fit into society. We learn to quieten our emotions, conceal what we are truly feeling, and we *lower our voices* to fit in with others. Through our conditioning and the suppression of our emotions, we quieten, piece by piece, our natural self. We begin to live a *quiet life*; nothing is allowed to disturb the peace. A *medium* level is the voice of reason; not too loud, not too quiet, somewhere in the centre is fine, just don't deviate too far.

No longer is there the *roar* of the child. With everything calm, or seemingly so, and no *visible ripples* on the lake of our life, the job has been done! The child no longer demonstrates his disquiet or his exuberance. Now he fits within the world of reason, respectability and what others might deem as *normality*.

The other day I had lunch with a good friend of mine. During our conversation he spoke effusively about his children, his son of 15 and his daughters of 8 and 9. He spoke lovingly about their accomplishments, how they all played musical instruments, his son mad on guitars and the girls being really into drama and dance.

He continued to tell me that one of his daughters had told him recently that she would love to be in the theatre, work in the arts; be an actress on the stage performing to an audience. My friend, whilst supportive of her, then spoke to me those worldly words *"it's nice for them to do these things as a hobby, but it's not a real job, she is doing really well at mathematics"*.

My friend has built up a great deal of personal wealth based upon *his definition* of what a real job is. He had worked real hard in the commercial world, the *real* world, and had been very nicely financially rewarded for his efforts. His definition was that dance, song, acting and music were great to do *hobbies*, a nice balance with academia, but academia is where reality is. It produces results that perceptibly lead to wealth and logically assured success.

In a world where the vast majority of people see the arts as for the chosen few, for the affluent society, or for the probably insane, to allow your child to follow that dream appears almost irresponsible.

My friend is in a financial position to support his daughter. He has the material wealth to allow her to follow her dream but will his definition of success, his belief in how the *real*-world works, allow him to see a wider picture?

I, like my friend, had followed the commercial path and I ran a similar business to him. However, where he thrived from the hustle and bustle of the business world, where he gained his joy and happiness in living this way, I suffered from stress, panic attacks, stomach disorders and massive fatigue!

At that time, I thought that we must all suffer in this same way. I reasoned that it went with the territory; was part of the job, part of the role where we had to pay the price for what we were doing. I reasoned that it was high pressure stuff, and I just didn't handle it very well, that was all. I justified my disorder to myself, that my anxiety, my feeling that something was intrinsically wrong, was related to my perpetual, long established self-doubt, relating to my abilities, skills and intelligence.

Having listened to my friends' recollection of his discussion with his daughter, I was moved to share a piece of my personal story with him, which I hoped could possibly open up his perspective and shift his interpretation of what he felt was best for his daughter.

I recalled to him that the only praise I received at school was for my written work. My essays and the stories I told showed an ability to paint a picture through words. I further informed him that, whilst I received this praise, no one ever encouraged me to utilise this innate gift as my future direction.

In addition, I did not come from a social background where anything like being a writer could even be contemplated or considered as a career. Writing is not easily defined as a job in the market place; especially not a job of value for someone from the masses!

I told him that no careers advisor ever asked me what my innate gifts were. No teacher ever took the time or encouraged me to follow this path. From my backyard, with my poor scholastic achievements, no value could be seen for a boy with this type of gift, as I needed to earn! I needed to contribute and survive in the only world that was seemingly on offer to me. Did he listen?

I completely comprehended where my friend was coming from regarding his daughters' future path. We hear it all the time. 'I will encourage her to get her qualifications first, gain something that will set her up for life, encourage her to keep her head down for a number of years, build a *real* career and then she can go back to her *dream* when she's established and can support herself.

In the world of *logic*, the world of *control*, the world of *reality*, this all makes perfect sense. Just one thing is missing. What happens to that individual in those interim years? What happens in those years of reason, of keeping their head down, of bending themselves out of shape, of denying their true desires of the life they dream to lead?

Yet more questions arose within me through that conversation. Is there a *definable* time or age for an individual to be at their peak? Is there a definable time or age where the individual blossoms into their full glory? How many people miss their *true time* due to the reasoning *reality* of the logical, *real* world? How easily can we miss our true calling in life through the *definition* of our *desire* by other people?

We hear stories of individuals who know precisely what their true purpose is. They know where their true bliss is to be found and they will not be shaken from this course by any other person or circumstance. Unfortunately, I believe these individuals are very rare beings. These people I consider extremely fortunate.

My friend has the financial resources to support his daughter in her chosen desire, but will he have the insight, the depth, the capacity, the awareness, the understanding, the humility and the love to allow her to follow a route that is alien to him? In essence, can he feel it within his heart to give her the chance to succeed or fail, or will logic prevail?

The pull of the material world is immensely powerful. After all, the basic life necessity is our need to feed ourselves, have clothing and shelter. For these things we need to earn money. In this logical world we secure a job and satisfy our basic needs. However, when only logic prevails, we become captured; we become restricted and limited in our vision by the workings of the logical mind. This logical mind of ours comprehends a structure, a defined, reasoned path that, if followed, will produce a tangible result.

In essence, as human beings we are prepared from our earliest age for the commercial world, in order to satisfy a list of responsibilities. These responsibilities are often defined as houses, family, food, holidays, cars, domestic appliances, entertainment. These responsibilities are paid for from the funds that we earn exchanging our time and skills for money.

Once we are captured in this logical, material world, we are perpetually *encouraged* to escalate ourselves up the social scale; to *better* ourselves, *display* our achievements. This escalation exponentially elevates the levels of responsibilities to be satisfied, thus requiring us to achieve ever improving levels of income to support this perceived social growth. A larger house, that high performance car, 79-inch TV with sound piped direct from source, 3 weeks holiday in a spa in Ecuador. This perpetual world of external goals and desires can only be satisfied by the constant exchange of our time and skill within the commercial world.

Can you remember a time when you had one of these external goals or desires? That dream home, that special holiday, that latest mobile phone? You felt *If Only* you could stretch that bit more, get to that goal, hold those keys in your hand, run your fingers through the sand, hear that ringing in your pocket, then yes, that would make you happy.

So, you stretch, and you get *there*. You have that look of satisfaction on your face. You have put yourself through some hardships to get to your goal, but now you have the prize! You can now tell everyone your goal has been attained!

But how long did that *feeling* last? A day, a week, perhaps even a month, though all too soon the euphoria, the excitement, the glow begins to fade. All too soon that external joy either becomes the norm or it starts to fade. Where once there was great pleasure, the excitement of attainment; the peak of satisfaction, all too soon the goal becomes your normality.

You become *accustomed* to your new acquisition. You become *normalised* to the way the car feels to drive. When you open the door no longer does that new car smell linger. You now *know* how it sounds as you turn the key. You don't look back at it so much when you walking to your front door. The goal has been attained, your desire met; but its attainment hasn't provided the lasting happiness you craved.

Now you need another fix, another goal, another plan to satisfy the insatiable, unquenchable thirst of the mind!

This model is the normality for the vast majority of human beings. The lottery win that will change everything! Most of us never stop this cycle. We go on looking for that one *external experience* that will provide lasting happiness. We keep searching for that external remedy which will finally satisfy the deep craving that calls inside for fulfilment. Surely it must to be *out there* somewhere?

Real, lasting happiness never comes from the outside. External stimulants give us a taste, a fleeting glimpse of the happiness we crave, but it fades as quickly as the first snowflake falling to the ground.

So why do we get trapped? Why do we lose track of where we should be heading? The core of our issues, the fulcrum of our discontent, revolves around the workings of the mind. The mind is a storage cabinet of our experiences. All of the events, traumas, delights, tragedies, beliefs, desires, our truth, our lies, are all held in this internal store. It is a compendium, an amalgam of all that has happened to us up until this point in space and time. The mind, however, is a part of who we are, an important, incredible part of who we are, but we must remember one thing; it is *not who we are!*

With the insatiable mind as our driver, we can never be lastingly happy, content or satisfied. We will never feel that we have reached our nirvana. We will continually search all our days for external satisfaction and that feeling of ease and appeasement. Through the mind alone we will never reach our truth.

I am not saying that the mind is not useful. It is an amazing gift that we have as humans. The mind is an incredible device in which vast amounts of detail, knowledge, skill and experience can be stored. It allows us to recall experiences that enable us to communicate, relate, console, express and empathise with others. It is a device that can be trained to learn new skills. It is a device that is never full and a device, which many of us know through its incessant chatter, is available 24/7! But again, I say; it is *not who we are!*

When our mind is *understood* as a device, an amazing tool to befriend, and is used as a gift to help us experience life in its totality, the mind is extraordinary. When the mind is *understood* as *us*, as *what we are*, as *the master,* as the *driver*, the mind is the curse of mankind.

It is a curse of epic proportion! The minds never ending search for lasting happiness through the external material world and the unquenchable resolution of retained experiences leaves us with perpetual feelings of longing and want.

Fortunately, we, the *Chosen Few*, reach a point along life's path where we realise that living through the limitations of the mind does not bring the contentment we desire. We reach a point where we instinctively, or perhaps more pertinently, intuitively know, there must be something more. There must be more than this cycle of idea, chase, experience, elation, dissatisfaction, idea....

At the stage where we realise the futility of our minds external search for happiness, many of us will have begun to suffer physical ailments. Bouts of depression, aching bones and limbs, stomach disorders, tooth and throat problems, panic attacks. We experience a host of ailments manifesting themselves through physical disorder. We are very often unaware however that the stimulus, the nucleus, the core of these physical disorders are psychological, not physical.

We treat these ailments through a variety of external treatments and distractors. We take Legal medication, illegal medication, anti-depressants, muscle relaxers, digestive suppressants, alcohol, work, sex, or whatever we believe could bring solution or at least suppression to the internal conflict and unrest that has become ignited within. These distractors turn us away from our intuitive need to look deeply into the fundamental, underlying issues we are facing.

The power of the human being is beyond any of our reasoned comprehension. Stimulated in certain ways, the human being can become three-fold stronger than normally perceived. A parent has been known to lift a car from their child who had become trapped underneath. These seemingly superhuman abilities do not come from thought, however; they do not come from the mind. They are stimulated through our experience and ignite a store of *inner resources.*

The experience triggers the body to respond and, as in the case of the parent lifting the car, the body releases stored, powerful chemicals which break the boundaries of our known belief systems. The unfolding event enables this previously untapped capability, power and resource, located within the body, to manifest and be released.

Disease of the physical body can often be an outcome of how our internal world is operating. Negative thoughts lead to negative feelings and emotions. These emotions unwittingly cause the body to release toxins and chemical messages through our bloodstream, stimulating the body to react in certain ways.

Think for a second about a real or created forthcoming stressful event. As an example, you are soon to meet up with a family member you fell out with 3 years ago and have not spoken to since. You felt they were criticising your side of the family for a situation that occurred many years before. This criticism had no truth from your perspective, but it had cast a shadow over the whole family ever since.

Now you are to meet this person again at a family wedding. You know they will be there. You know the day is supposed to be a happy one for the bride and groom, yet you cannot stop thinking of how the words this person said made you feel inside. You feel enraged, tearful, dumbstruck and hurt that someone could actually think and say those things.

How does your body feel now? The person is not actually here; yet their voice resounds in your ears, their words etched within your mind. Your shoulders tense, your breathing shortens, your legs feel heavy not wanting to move. Your chest feels tight, your tongue is dry; your back aches between the shoulder blades. Yet who is there? No one is there in physical form, but though the innate, unknowable power of the human being, they are.

Now, take this type of scenario, with its associated feelings and manifestations, and add it to all the other unresolved issues you carry around on a daily basis. Lay these issues one on top of another. Each layer has a cumulative impact upon your physical health; yet these physical feelings, these external ailments, are all being triggered by psychological remembrances carried inside of *your mind.*

When we retain and carry these layered remembrances, in some cases for many years, the pain and physical distress we feel becomes our norm. We get used to it. Our system begins to adjust, it accepts that this way of feeling is our *normality* and is how we *normally* feel on a daily basis. We have built another skill within the mind; a skill in pain management. This pain becomes our *normality* and thus defines *who we are today.*

Our mind continually turns over these accumulated thoughts and experiences, experiences that are very often negative in content. Our mind plays the same movie over and over, but it constantly seeks to find a different ending! It plays that same movie which is already written, filmed, released and experienced; but it doesn't like the ending! It continually tries to change something that has already happened. Without our *conscious* intervention, we continually seek different answers and different resolutions to the situations and circumstances we have experiences.

The greatest damage is caused by these accumulated layered experiences when we try to resolve why something has happened to us. Why did our relationship go wrong? Why did I not stay on that extra year to complete my education? Why did I have such a poor relationship with my father? Why do I always feel I have no money? Why am I always overlooked when work promotions come around? Why did my mother push me towards that secretarial course rather than that art degree which would have transformed my life? Why didn't I follow my heart to become a professional footballer rather than listen to the logic of my father to get a real job and then do my hobby? Why oh why have I been so stupid?

 A critical point to remember is ***Our Mind Knows Only What It Knows!*** For us to move forward we must comprehend the principle that *Our Mind* is *Our Mind* alone. No one else will ever have this storage cabinet we call the mind. No one else will have had our upbringing, our learning or the experiences we have encountered during our life so far.

As a young child we view the world through unfiltered eyes. Everything we experience is digested by our mind and is stored as a fact. It accepts everything as *how things are*; *how they should be, how this is normality for us*. These early years thus create our initial *reality*; they create our early social norm.

As we grow, more and more knowledge and information crosses our horizon. This additional information is stored alongside the previous knowledge that has been consumed. Often the information received surrounds the same subject, but now it has a different, more intricate flavour. The experience is added to, it now has more breadth and additional layers to support the subject. It has more detail upon which a belief on that particular subject can be built, consumed, embedded and further substantiated.

As an example, at an early age we were criticised for *not being good* at remembering details on subjects we were taught. We could remember that Penicillin is used to fight bacteria in the body, but we couldn't fully remember the name of the man who discovered it. Furthermore, we were not sure of the year it was discovered, though we thought it was 1929.

Then we experience upsetting our favourite aunt by forgetting the date of her birthday. At school meanwhile, we were still struggling through the curricula, trying desperately to remember those detailed facts about subjects we were taught just 2 days before.

A belief is now established. These *events* begin to support the perspective that we are not academic. The message we now start to give ourselves is that we're not competent, and most certainly we're not intelligent! The original, faint belief has now been compounded, and is substantiated by these consecutive events. We now start to *place ourselves* within a hierarchy of intelligence across our peer group. A *Foundational Brick* has now been removed from our *Wall of Self Esteem*. A new inscription has been written upon one of our bricks and has been placed back within our *Wall of Self Esteem,* as a *statement of fact*!

With this brick firmly installed and substantiated within our *Wall of Self Esteem,* we begin to feel inferior to others on a conscious and/or subconscious level. More and more *supportive examples* come our way to embed the belief, a belief that becomes entrenched as a part of us, a characteristic of us, *it becomes us.*

Now, every time we are asked to recall a detail or fact, we react in a limiting way, and trigger an automatic response. We trigger a voice inside that shouts "you fool, you can't remember because you are so stupid, you're not very intelligent are you!"

The answer is often there, but the answer is now trying to claw its way through an interwoven web of self-doubt; a deep swamp of accumulated experiences shouting that you lack the ability to remember. This belief, this habit, is not only written; it is etched and deeply engraved through repetition by an iron fist, into the structure of your mind.

Our mind is an accumulation of *our own* experiences and *our own* translation of these experiences. When we become aware and can comprehend this as a fundamental fact, we become empowered with an understanding of immense significance. Through the awareness of our own consciousness, we have the ability to reform and restructure the *experiential beliefs* we hold!

You now hold another Master Key for your future. This is the first stage of *your responsibility*. This Master Key opportunity enables you to **Review, Refresh and Befriend non-helpful content of your mind.**

The cleansing of the mind is a deep, cathartic process which requires your total commitment, dedication, determination, desire, understanding, and *complete trust*.

This cleansing process could be described as *re-creating the vessel to enable you to set sail towards your freedom.* You will be free from the shackles of the mind. You will be free from constantly searching to change a *fact* that has happened to you. You will be free from your past and its ability to drain and sap your life energy. This is a massive step, but there is more, so much more!

Without the past constantly dragging you backwards by the hair, you become free to experience your future with awe. This new future, however, will not just be a sticking plaster version of your past. No; through this deep cleansing, you are free to discover what life itself wants to bring to you.

If you consider yourself to be only your mind, you are an island. You are surrounded by a deep dangerous sea, where you feel isolated, marooned and alone in the world. To live with joy, you must allow yourself to once again be like a child, though this child now has the gift of wisdom. When once again you become innocent, clean and fresh, you become open to allow life to work on you for a change!

You need immense courage to be totally true to your authentic self; the self you were before you took on the lessons of the crowd. Your authentic self communicates to you what is right and wrong for you as an individual spirit. It is *your-self*, based upon the truths and desires which harmonise and resonate with your being and your emotions at any point in time. You must re-discover and re-write what was originally written upon those bricks within your *Wall of Self Esteem*.

As you review your past, understand it and say *"aha, you really had me fooled there,"* you need to remain consciously aware of a fundamental trap. If you begin to replace your old world with a new set of fixed beliefs, you will only have moved so far. You may operate in a different way, perhaps an improved way, but it will still be a defined, consistent and restrictive way. You will again be subject to reacting to a specific situation in a robotic, mechanical manner, based upon these new beliefs you have embedded into your wall.

With a mind clean of formulated belief structures, you can lead a life of spontaneity! A spontaneous life is a life of flow. You respond to any given situation naturally and independently, in that present moment. It is a life not based upon re-action; it is a response to the specific instance and the specific moment in time.

Consider with me. You have a belief, either formed by yourself, through the family, social perception or religion, that you will never have a one-night stand. You have never had one and have never found yourself in this situation. You believe you would feel dirty, unreligious, cheap, and lacking discipline.

You know that your principle is based upon sound ground, sound intelligence and sound reasoning. You believe it will be applauded by all of those around. You will be able to say, "I stood firm, I followed my script, I lived my training".

Then it happens. The possibility of a one-night stand comes incomprehensively into your life. Now it is not a theoretical construct; this situation is real. The other person is looking deep into your eyes. 'This is mad; we only met an hour ago, though every part of my being desires to experience this totally unexpected situation'. You are swept along by emotions that overwhelm the power of your logical mind. The energy you feel has a thrill that you have never experienced before.

Your formalised beliefs shout at you to walk away. Your reason, your logical mind insists you must do the *right thing*. You evaluate that you must remain true to your long-held beliefs. You consider that you must take pride in yourself by taking this stand but, from somewhere deep down inside, a voice is screaming at you to experience the fire of this desire. Is this voice *us*, is it *our inner voice*, or is it the master that's our mind?

When we are free from our past conditioning, we will make the right decision based totally in that present moment of time. The decision we take will be the *true you* 'calling', and not the voice of the crowd.

You may ask, "If I live my life totally at the mercy of each individual moment in time, how will I know how to be? How will I know who I am? How will I know how to behave and be accepted by others?" How will I know that I should open myself to these experiences?

 These questions are based upon control. Once again, *your mind* needs to *know*. It won't let you rest. Here now lays another crucial point; ***Trust Your Self.***

You must trust yourself with utter confidence. You must trust and release your inner being, your inner guide, your inner self. *Your Self* will take care of your every need at any specific moment in time. Your inner guide will navigate you through any waters. You may never have responded before to how it is guiding you at that specific moment; yet the pleasure gained through this *trust* is immeasurable.

With no pre-judgement, with no predetermination, with no pre-emption of outcome; you can live a life of response and intense excitement towards every experience you encounter. If you are brave and have the courage to stand tall, if you are willing to risk your whole past, you can encounter a way of being which is based upon *experiencing life lived spontaneously*. A life lived with no set map, with no revisited destinations and with no set beliefs or limitations. Living in this way, there is nothing to suppress or restrict your ability to enjoy your life to its maximum, a life which is presented daily to your table.

My question to you now is this. Are you ready to choose?

Experiences

Personal Review

- How happy do you feel? How are you measuring this?

- How much encouragement have you received during your life so far? How has this affected you doing what you desire or desired to do?

- How influenced do you feel you are by what you have been taught in the past? How do these influences impact upon your day to day behaviour? What are your thoughts surrounding the Master Key that states *Our Mind Knows Only What It Knows!*

- When you think about your past experiences how do they make you feel? Can you feel the changes in your body chemistry? How do they make you feel? How do they affect your day?

- Do you feel you re-act to situations or respond? Do situations seemingly keep resurfacing, perhaps in another disguise but are allied to the same subject?

- How is your health? Do you feel relaxed or stressed? How would you know?

- Are there recurring thoughts that you have which stimulate you to feel stressed or anxious or distressed? What are they?

- What issues are you always trying to resolve or find a different ending to in your mind?

- How helpful would it be to be able to *Review, Refresh and Befriend non-helpful content of your mind?*

- What unhelpful thoughts or beliefs about yourself do you repeatedly have?

- How much do you *Trust Your Self*? How much do you *Trust your own judgement*?

Remember, this is all good. You are here for a reason.

You have the potential to live the life you were born to lead.

Chapter 3   *Choose Your Future*

Scales of Decision

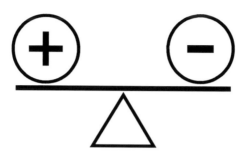

How will I know when I choose this crazy life, how will I know what I choose will be right, how will I know

How can I grow when all I feel is fright, how many times must I choose wrong from right, how will I know

How many times must I be asked to decide, to choose my path though these eyes are totally blind

To open my arms to a world that is free and so warm, to finally find that place that I can always call home

How will I know

When you begin to see the dawn, and realise what is going on in the world, or more succinctly; within *your* world, you reach a crossroads. As you examine the way in which you have been experiencing and interpreting everything that has happened to you, you arrive at a point of decision. You reach a position where you have the power to make a fundamental life choice.

You have the power to choose to take the quality and pleasure of your life into your own hands. You have the power to choose whether to take *total responsibility*, those words again, for how you experience every minute, day, week or year. You also have the power to choose to let what could be an amazingly beautiful, ecstatic, purposeful, liberating, loving, invigorating life slip through your fingers.

The choices, decisions and level of responsibility you take define your future. There is no greater responsibility. There is no greater courage. There is no greater potential than the one which comes to you on this day of reckoning. Our day of reckoning is not the one served on our death bed. Our day of reckoning comes at the point where life provides us with the chance, the opening and the opportunity to choose the way we are going to live our future life.

However, to enable us to live in accord with our intrinsic nature, the level and degree of changes we make can be of such magnitude that we may become *unrecognisable* from the person who used to walk the same street. People may say, "I know the face, I know how they used to be, how they always appeared to be, but now, somehow, they are different; something must have happened to them!"

We also must be prepared that these changes may not be in accord with the interests of others. The changes that occur, the changes that enable us to harmonise with our intrinsic nature, can take us headlong into conflict with both ourselves and the societal norms to which we have been subject up to this point.

The decisions and choices you decide to take, often fundamental changes, can reveal the true magnificence of your individuality. They can allow you to taste the fulfilment of your personal destiny; they can transform the way you walk along that same street.

No longer are you wearing that social mask you wore before. You now smile a wholehearted, deep, genuine, integrated smile that others *know* comes from deep inside. Before, you were the wall flower, never taking centre stage. You never said what you really felt. Deep down you knew what you had to say was as valid, as relevant, as interesting as anything the others had to say, but you kept quiet. You lacked the courage, the inner belief, the self-esteem, because the outside world had imprinted in you *their* version of how the world works. But look at you now!

You now have the beginnings of awareness as to why you are searching for answers to the way you feel. You now have the opportunity to never again betray yourself. My challenge to you is this; *are you prepared for this?*

At the highest peak of remembering the *True You*, you will experience a situation called *Choice-less Choice*. *Choice-less Choice* is where you flow with life, you allow and trust natures' guidance to lead and direct you forward without any resistance to its message. You become that spontaneous creature, open to each and every moment and act in accord with what is correct in that specific moment of time.

However, at this early stage of *transformation*, you must utilise *Conscious Choice* to begin the process. You *consciously* must choose to *think differently.* You *consciously* must *behave* in a different way. You *consciously* must *respon*d, and you need to *consciously interpret* the world in a different way.

To begin this process of *transformation*, you must use your *conscious mind* to choose your response to every situation. For most of us, many, many years have been lived within the confines of deep conditioning that have defined our lives. Years of inaction, years of personal denial, years of living under the guidance of others have all to be systematically and sympathetically evaluated, understood and healed. By releasing the power of the *conscious mind,* you enable the most important forward steps of your life to begin.

You must *consciously* take full control. You have to climb into the driving seat and grip that steering wheel hard. Your examination test is about to start. You may begin to shake and consider; how much do I want this freedom? How much do I want to free myself to go where I want to go and not be reliant upon anyone else for a lift? No more hitching a ride, no more going at *their* pace, no more having to take *their* chosen route. But hang on a minute, this test sounds like hard work?

 Can you recall the effort you had to invest in order to pass something like that driving test? Can you recall the tightness you felt in every limb as you trembled at each junction? Can you remember the way you had to keep talking to yourself to calm your inner turmoil? Can you relive how you *consciously* had to remember to move your head to ensure that the examiner could see that you were looking in thew rear-view mirror? That level of remembrance is called **conscious choice.**

At the stage of *conscious choice*, you have to review your own distinctions surrounding what is wrong, what is right, what's good, what's bad, what empowers you and what saps your energy. You consciously have to move through the situation where for so long you have been subjected to a way of thinking and to the conditioning of others.

To look at how deeply conditioning seeps into our bloodstream, let's take a subject such as sex. Sex is beautiful, sex is cathartic, sex is liberating, yet sex is perhaps one of the most taboo subjects to speak about, especially within the family setting. The Catholic Church, even to this day, will not formally recognise contraception. How can such an institution be so naive; or is it far from naivety? Is there perhaps a method supporting their seemingly prehistoric stance on the subject of contraception?

Having experienced a Catholic upbringing, my now interpretation of their portrayal of sex is one of hypocrisy. The virgin bride creates the perspective that we should only have sex to produce children. Priests and Nuns are married to the order. They remain celibate to their calling, devout to their constant requirement to do good deeds.

Natures' instruction, however, is to procreate. It is a phenomenon that naturally occurs in most people. This desire is not intellectual. We can make a conscious choice or decision to not participate, to not follow our instincts, to suppress this natural desire, but we must fully understand that nature itself is communicating this message. It is an inborn, bodily instinct that is the driver.

How often, however, is this natural delight spoken of within the family circle? How many parents, even today, really talk openly about the delights of making love? Do we share what we should be aware of, how to gain maximum pleasure, how to please each other? Do we describe why making love between two consenting people can be the most amazing experience? I believe there are possibly three core reasons why the sharing of one of life's most beautiful experiences is so rare.

Handed from generation to generation, many of us as parents do not have a deep, open relationship with our child that would allow such a conversation. We may never have truly spoken from the heart together. We may never have exposed our own frailties, our own concerns, our own limiting beliefs, or shared such deep experiences. We may never have had the courage to speak with our own flesh and blood on such a deep intimate level.

This level of communication would require us to speak to our children on an adult to adult basis. Then the mind of the *parent* intercedes, 'if we reveal ourselves in this way, what would our child think? Will the illusion we have created over so many years be shattered? Will they see us in the same way?

Will they still *respect* us, even when it might appear that we do not even know ourselves?'

Another reason may well surround the possibility that we as the parent have never experienced for ourselves the delight of a deep, fully intense intimacy. How could we authentically share an experience when it is not from our own autobiography? We would be speaking from the perspective of hypothesis, from something that is possible, though it is a perspective that is not proven or the *known* of the communicator. After all, we don't want to lie to our children so best avoid this type of subject, just guide them towards the practicalities as our parents did for us. Yet consider for a moment. Hand me down clothes can only be used so many times. At some point they become so frayed, so tattered so threadbare that they need a radical replacement.

Perhaps, however, the third reason is the most potent. Deep, debilitating messages are sent through religious and other forms of education as to the perils of the human flesh. Could it be that these *educators* know there is amazing pleasure to be experienced through the intimacy of two people?

Could it be they know that if individuals knew how to achieve such pleasure for themselves, pleasure without any feeling of remorse or wrong doing, then rather than heed the call of the church bell for salvation, they might decide they do not need the church anymore? Just some more thoughts to ponder over!

When you suppress anything within it appears somewhere else. If you declare that you will no longer eat cake you will see cake everywhere! You decide to go on a diet; what happens? All you think about, all you crave, all you desire is food. You can see it; you can even hear it as it sizzles in the pan! The power of the mind, especially where suppression is its embodiment, is powerful indeed.

Living in an unconscious way, you remain a victim to circumstance. You remain a victim to your environment and to your concept of how life is dealing its cards. Your winning hand is dealt when you decide to take *total responsibility* and *choose* your own direction.

So why do so few of us choose this course? Why are most people living at the lowest possibility of happiness and freedom? I believe it is because, to the vast majority of people, they believe there is no other way.

'This is it. These are the cards I have been dealt'. They have no awareness of

their situation or, if they are aware, when they look into the abyss they call their life and know that they must take full responsibility for what they see, they run for cover and plunge their head straight into the sand!

Awareness can be described as the *conscious exposure of how you are currently living*. Awareness is within the realisation that there are alternative ways to think, feel, experience and be. However, even with this new-found awareness, fear can strike the seeker rigid. As you begin to become more aware of your options you fear you may choose incorrectly. You fear you might make further *mistakes* and these *mistakes* could now be of a far higher magnitude and what's more, you will have no one to blame, but yourself!

In this world it is rare to come across someone who will *truly* encourage you to reach for the stars. Mostly we are encouraged to stay close to the shore we know. A cautious, reasoned approach is recommended. Stay *safe* so that when the tide comes in you will know how long it will take to reach the shore of security.

In this way you remain in control. The horizon is where you have always known it be, your environment is defined, clear and understood. You now cannot go wrong as you *know* where the *shore* is. Yet you are intrinsically aware this *shore* is where you have been stranded for oh! so long.

Imagine setting foot on an unknown shore. What do you *know?* No longer can you rely upon *your memory*, upon *your knowing*. Suddenly, you have no option but to be alive to what is happing in each and every moment. Your senses have to be acutely tuned, as the territory before you is *unknown*. Never before have you seen this place. It could be filled with the riches of danger or pleasure, the amount of which we know not; yet through the intensity of the *unknown* you are truly alive! Everything is fresh, it has to be. You are no longer in control, you cannot control the *unknown*, yet now your pulse will rise, your awareness on high alert.

Choice is often wild. When you begin again to listen to your instinct, when you experience your intuition, when you trust your innate vision of your life's desires, your choices may be diametrically opposed to the logical instructions of your mind!

 This point must be deeply understood. The mind is and will remain security conscious. The mind wants to control, it wants to be in charge; it wants to be the master. It wants to safeguard you from the perils that it perceives may lie ahead. You need to prepare yourself for an *inner civil war*. Your mind verses your most ***fundamental elements of instinct, intuition and trust.***

The Key *fundamental elements* are very often *non-logical*. They do not *fit* with where you are. They are not practical, they are not *thought out*. They are not constrained by safety, yet they are yours all the same! Others may describe them as *gut reactions* or *dream land*. They may say *"Yes, enjoy your dreams; enjoy your little escape from reality, and then just get real, we all have to!"* Even if someone does have the capacity to go along with our little dream, they encourage us to look into the future and attempt the non-attainable ability to try and work out all possible scenarios that you may encounter. But how can you think about something you do not know? How can you *think* about something you have never encountered or experienced?

How can you know what it will be like to ride that surfboard on the open sea? You can use your mind to visualise what you perceive it might be like. You can imagine the chill of the water. You can arrange the ingredients to allow you to participate; the ability to swim, the ability to balance on the board, the wet weather clothing, the location and who could help you achieve the experience. Yes, the mind can help tremendously with the practicalities of your desire, but it does not create the desire, or deliver the experiencing of the experience itself. Only through your awareness comes possibility. Awareness opens the *door to possibility*!

The *door to possibility* enables incredible perspective and awareness through the choices you are presented with. Yet these possibilities of choice are often conflicting to the comprehension of the baying crowd.

 The element which sits upon the same shelf as *choice* is **Total Responsibility.** One of the most fundamental failures of the individual is the non-acceptance that you are *totally responsible* for the quality of your life. There is no greater responsibility. When you reach critical points within your lifetime, the ownership of your responsibilities is central to your ability to move forward.

Responsibility at this point comes in two parts. Firstly, you need to become fully aware of your situation. You need to become fully *conscious* of the way you are currently living and fully aware of the denial you have endured for so long. This examination of your current world leads naturally to the second part where you must take total responsibility to expose and follow your *true path*. For so long you have denied or suppressed the existence of this path, but now your heart is calling you back; and nature will often intervene and take the initiative to powerfully signal its call!

When nature intervenes' to move us towards another path, our emotional turmoil and consequential physical distress is raised to an acute level. When the emotional pain felt is of sufficient intensity, such that we can take no more, nature will have taken control! Nature will have manifested a situation, or a number of situations, where we have no alternative but to review and choose a different direction.

For example, imagine you are in an abusive relationship. Your daily diet contains servings of aggression, negativity, spite and stress. On a *normal* day you can just about stand the atmosphere. The violence, after all, is emotional not physical. You know deep down inside that things are not good, but you compensate; you *suppress* those *knowing* feelings.

You pacify yourself with delusional, reasoned thoughts. *"They are just going through a difficult time, though I do wonder how many years a difficult time can be! I'm sure they will turn themselves around soon. They will see the light; they will take responsibility for their behaviour like they always say they will. After all, what I am experiencing is the same as I see daily in my favourite soap on the TV. All families are the same. After the initial excitement of meeting and getting to know each other things go like this, what else should I expect, just ask all my friends, they will tell you! And after all, where else could I go?"*

One day however, the other totally loses it, they hit you. This has never happened before. The dynamic within the relationship has now totally changed. The situation has reached a different level!

The final act in what you called a relationship has now been performed. Now, because of this escalation to physical abuse, you will take no more. There can be no more chances, no more excuses. The cord is cut. The emotions you have suppressed for so long erupt and culminate into a point of decision. The choice is made.

Yet, can you see how *nature* has taken the call? Something *outside* intervened to bring you to a point of decision. On your own you could not decide, you continued to *bend* to the situation, so *nature* created and *escalated* the level of pain to force the issue.

However, was it right that *nature* had to be called upon to conspire to move this situation to such a critical point, a point where there was no option but to act? How much duress and distress must be experienced before the individual will take their responsibility and decide what is right? This person had known for so long that the relationship had been worthless; it was no way to live a life. Yet they didn't have the courage or strength to accept responsibility and act upon what they knew deep inside was wrong. What was it about them that allowed this situation to continue? Was it perhaps their *self-worth* that was on trial here?

Secretly, did they feel, consciously or unconsciously, that this was all someone like them should expect of life? Did they feel worthy of a loving, happy, beautiful relationship? How did they really see themselves? Yes, the other party had their issues, but those were *their* issues.

Why did this person allow the situation to reach such a peak of discomfort, accept the emotional and mental abuse, before they were forced into making a decision? What was it about *them* that allowed things to go on for so long until *nature* had to intervene to lead the way?

Their internal guidance system had been informing them for so long as to the perils of the situation they were in. It kept on *telling* them that they were in the wrong place, on the wrong shore; with the wrong person. They knew they were not living the beautiful life they had dreamt of as a child. Their stomach turned every time they looked at the clock that counted down to the other party's return. Their sleeping pattern suffered massively as constant, debilitating thoughts ran through their mind.

Their diet was poor as the foods they could eat that didn't upset their stomach were few. When they looked in the mirror they wondered who the person was staring back at them. Those guiding voices inside just wouldn't release their torment. They told them constantly the steps to take; but something always stopped them.

The *Fear of the unknown* traumatises mankind like no other force. This person knew the relationship was no good, but they always considered; how do I know the next will be any better?

The job we hate is numbing our mind, destroying our soul; but we have a mortgage to pay, a family to feed, the children want to go to university in the future so how can we change? We justify the situation to ourselves. 'The children will be off our hands in 10 years' time and then I'll make the change'. 'I will travel the world when I retire'. 'I know my legs say go now but that's just me being stupid. The right way to live, as the intelligent people say, is get that great education, work hard, pay off the mortgage, build a pension, save money and then I can do that travelling when I retire; yes, that's the correct order'.

I say, if you have a voice inside that is calling to you today; a voice screaming at you as you read this, then *you* had better listen!

Alternatively, take this action. Get a pen and a piece of paper and write down how your whole life will unfold. Document how it will all work out. Detail how everything will go in accordance to your / their model for your life of 'education, work, strive, pay, save, retire then play', and furthermore, note the actual date you will die. If you can do this, I bow down and salute you!

For you have in your hands *the holy grail of life*, and you are worth a fortune! You must be able to see into the future like no other. You must have a greater knowing than anyone who has ever walked this earth. Yes, you must have more insight than Jesus! Do you think he knew he would only get 33 years of life? Do you think he could foresee that he would have only four years to spread his words to the world? This is the same length of career as Jimi Hendrix, interesting eh!

The people who are satisfying their own needs will *provide us* with a template for how to live our life. For instance, how deeply have you thought that a mortgage, without an *aware knowing eye*, captures us in its bondage of financial exchange for 20 to 30 years!

It is suggested that the stress we encounter in this fast-moving world, the discomfort, the striving, the pushing, with its impact upon our physical health, is normal of life today. The picture is painted that when we reach that designated age where our pension will be released, we will be able to enjoy all the fruits of our labours. But tell me something. At 65 or 70 do you believe you will be 'able' to do all those activities that you could have done in your prime?

"Now, just hang on a minute" I hear you scream! *"Life doesn't work like that. You can't have everything! We have to follow the path and accept that when we*

are in our prime we need to be working, striving and stretching every sinew for that time when I can retire!"

Do you see the game? Have those light bulbs started to illuminate? Is there a glimmer of a smile coming to the side of your mouth as you realise what has been going on? It is very rare that anyone sees the game. When I first began to see it, I denied it completely. How could I have been so easily manipulated? How could others do this to me when I *believed* they had my best interests at heart, not theirs!

Choice and *Total Responsibility* walk hand in hand. Choice and responsibility provides us with *freedom* and opportunity, though whilst walking with this freedom, *fear* will be our constant companion!

Imagine a fearful scenario, perhaps a monstrous fairground ride? Time and time before you had walked up to that pay booth to take that ride, yet time and time again you had walked away.

This time though, for some unfathomable reason, you are transfixed. You can visualise how you might feel afterwards, you tremble as you perceive how intense it will be to fly into the sky. However, as you stand there shaking, with the fare money gripped in your hand, the ride remains just that; a vision, a perception. It is still a projection, a construction made within your mind; a picture of *what might be*. Once again you walk towards that pay booth, but this time you see your hand placing the money into your tormentors' hands!

Your legs feel weak through your projected fear of what is to come. All too soon you are at the front of the queue and now there is nowhere to run, turning away is not an option! *They strap you in tight. The mechanisms clunk into action. Every sense in your body is on full alert. Your palms sweat, your heart beats through your temples. You smell the oil of the machine as it slowly, almost painfully, winches you into position. Everything stops. Only sheer darkness confronts your eyes. You can't breathe, you want to escape; your tongue goes dry. Suddenly the full force of the pent-up mechanism thrusts you into the distance! Through daring to decide to actually experience this projected vision, your constructed fears transform into ecstasy. You scream, you roar, your body shakes with excitement; you experience the adrenalin pouring through every sinew.*

Far too quickly, you reach the end of the ride. Now there is no fear, no dread is felt. You had finally found the courage to walk to that pay booth. You paid the price for the thrill, and such a thrill. No longer is it just a vision, a perhaps it will be like.... now it's your personal experience. You faced your fear and still walked on. You now explicitly know how that experience feels. It is an *experience* you will always carry with you; it is now part of you. You have placed yet another decisive brick back into your *Wall of Self Esteem*.

You had choice. You could have walked away, as you had so many times before. You could have stopped at that pay booth and left with that same old feeling. You could have continued to hear that same condescending, internal voice, screaming 'still chicken then, always was, always will be!'

Someone told me recently how, on her wedding day, she *knew* the marriage she was about to enter was a mistake. Deep down she knew she was not *in love* with the man she was about to share her life with, to say those words to; to lay beside every night.

She told me she spoke to her sister and brother in law on that day about her dilemma. As is so often the case in these situations, they provided *the right* comforting words at the time. "Everything will be fine; it's only natural to feel nervous, everyone gets the wobbles. Get out there girl and smile for the cameras. The whole family is coming; you can't let them down now".

Fifty years later she is telling her story. The story of how she *knew* she was right. The story of how she had never experienced a deep, loving relationship she so desired. Her story recounted continual challenges, conflicts, struggles, and the worst part of it all, her own *self*-denial.

To her *self* she justified her *story* with the belief regarding family shame or rejection if she had decided to follow her *inner voice*. She went through with that wedding and continues to this day to compromise her life.

On that day she had been presented with a choice that would affect her whole life. What would her life have been if she had chosen differently? She will never know. She can dream, she can justify, she can distract her mind, yet, at that critical time, her inner voice had called to her 'what if........?'

I found this story so sad. For the *greater good* they had continued with what appeared the *right* thing to do, and had made the best of what they had chosen, but really; what might have been their *other life's story?*

Our heart is our inner guide, not the logical mind. The heart's power of decision is one thousand times stronger than a decision reached within the mind. The heart is all knowing, it is undeniable. It does not speak with logic, it speaks with energy. It communicates with a power stronger than the burning sun. It speaks with a power which is non-negotiable.

Will the choices you take always be right, or could they be wrong? Who knows; but by listening to the calling of your heart, and by taking *Total Responsibility* for your choice, you now empower and determine the direction.

You can review and alter the heading at any time. The direction chosen by you may appear absurd to others and to your own *logical* mind. Through the fullness of time, however, you will look back on the decisions led by your heart and find that your heart has guided you towards a magnificent horizon.

 When navigating towards your true world, there will be many stops and alterations of your course, as the journey cannot be taken in one step. However, with your heart as the guiding master, you now have another tool to use, the ability to ***choose and alter your course according to your heart.***

A rudderless boat lost at sea is a disaster waiting to happen. The sea is wild, it's unpredictable; yet it is also fresh, alive, vibrant and filled with life. Sometimes the sea is calm, sometimes it's stormy, but if you take the responsibility to choose your path and steer utilising the directions of your heart; you can navigate any sea and transcend any eventuality that life may present to you.

Choose Your Future

Personal Review

- You must use **Conscious Choice** to change long held beliefs. Have you examples you can recall where you have used *conscious choice* to change something in your life before? What were the results?

- How *free* within your current circumstances do you feel? What is it that holds you back from feeling *free*? What would *freedom* mean to you?

- How *safe* are you living? What would happen if you felt you were in uncharted territory?

- What level of **Total Responsibility** are you currently taking for your life? How are you measuring this?

- What are you putting up with that you *know* you shouldn't? What does this say about you?

- Have you made decisions that were the *logically right* things to do, though your insides and your heart were telling you differently? What were they? What were the outcomes?

- How in tune with your **Instinct, Intuition& and Trust** are you? How would you know?

- How brave do you think and feel you are?

- To what level are you letting your heart guide you rather than your reasoning mind?

- If you were able to completely choose the life of your dreams, to *alter your course in line with your heart*, how close currently are you to that dream? What is your dream? What are the gaps? What is not being fulfilled?

Remember, this is all good. You are here for a reason.

You have the potential to live the life you were born to lead

Chapter 4   *Limiting Beliefs*

A dawning of an age it is before us, a knowledge not born of books and say

People are finding they are people, Born to be free and that's okay 'If Only' we can see it, the games they like to play

Controlling every moment, till we don't know our own way

Imagine the scene. You are talking to a work colleague at lunchtime. They ask you for your opinion regarding the meeting you both had attended the day before. At the meeting the business had communicated their desire to change the daily working hours. The company believed the changes would provide a better service for their customers. Your colleague specifically wanted to know what you thought about their contribution at the meeting, the quality of what they had said, and how they came across to the others who were present.

You respond that you thought the points they had raised were very valid, although you also thought that they had come across a bit aggressively.

Suddenly, you are confronted with a face of fury. *"How dare you criticise what I have to say. You don't know how difficult it is for me to organise my kids and my life to fit in with the hours we currently work. It's alright for you. You've got your life sorted, what with your new car, your holidays abroad and your education. I have worked so hard to get to my position in this company, but you wouldn't understand that would you"*!

'Where the hell did that come from,' you wonder as you reel back in shock. You had only given your honest opinion and had done what your colleague had asked from you, yet now you are being served with a torrent of spiteful venom. The venom thrown at you feels totally unjustified, completely out of context and has left you truly bewildered.

Unwittingly, you had tapped into the other persons *Volcano of Past*. You had pierced a stream of molten lava which you had no idea existed. You exposed a seam, a fissure, a weak spot, which then poured its molten mass onto an innocent host. You opened up a channel of suppressed angers, beliefs, disappointments and frustrations which were all released from their prison when the pressure inside reached crisis point.

Our past events, stored with deep seated emotional ties, lie simmering inside, and are stirred continually by daily happenings. These past events are perpetually added to with associated examples, and become as hard as rock, forming into mountainous boulders of *belief*.

Over time, our inherent gifts and attributes become mixed and entangled as we consume more and more experiences through our encounters with the *outside world*. The understanding of how these two fundamental elements of our essence combine, enables us to realise why no one else on earth will see the world as we do. It will never happen. We may take, or have already taken, years trying to convince others of our exact point of view regarding our experiences or events. Others can *empathise* with the way we see it, but the other will still see *their* picture; *their* associations, *their* understanding and *their* interpretation of the described experience or event.

As a child we have none of these entanglements. As life progresses we begin to be exposed to and gather experiences or events. These events begin to form together and consequentially they create *our history*.

Unfortunately for the human being, by far the most powerful remembrances of these stored experiences and events appear to be negative in nature. We *learn* to become *safety conscious* through our experiences. We *learn* not to go near the fire; we *learn* not to run into the road, we *learn* to look where we are going and take care when we are holding things. Often these *learning's* are gained the hard way, through our experiences!

As we grow, the way in which we *perceive* the world begins to be shaped by the memories stored within our mind. These memories and recollections produce a unique template, a unique set of eyes and a unique human being. This collective produces a *unique reaction* to the world. What has occurred to us in the past now creates a unique reaction to our present and future. When we are unconscious to this understanding, we react to the world through a reconstruction of our past.

So why do we as human beings retain these experiences and events, especially the ones which are damaging, destructive, disempowering and de-motivational? These memories can be debilitating and are often just downright awful. So why can't we just decide to erase them from our memory banks, clean our canvas and replace them with a happy picture to frame?

I believe the mind *stores everything* that we experience throughout our lives. It stores events which were happy, sad, good or bad. It stores experiences which were encouraging, discouraging, stressful or full of peace.

These cumulative events and experiences become bound together and are then reinforced by psychological ties which *emotionalise* the event. Thus, a massive bond is created with our experiences and events and they become hard wired into the brain. These emotional connections reveal why powerful negative events are all too easily remembered.

The negative event has a massive impact within our memory bank. A child returns to the fire with extreme caution once they have experience the intensity of getting too close to the flame. The screaming pitch of a concerned parent, at the critical point of danger, indelibly writes the event or experience into the reference library of the child's mind.

 Here is a massive challenge to you. As part of your ability to move forward, to *Resurrect & RECLAIM the True You* and *gain your Prize*, I encourage you to move towards a new way of viewing your history. The challenge lies within the requirement to accept that **the mind remembers everything as a Fact.** It is remembered to provide us with critical information at the requisite time.

We hear stories of people, following a significant trauma where they came close to their death, who can recall that their whole life's story of events and experiences flashed before them. They are left with the revelation that their life's story had been projected like a film before their eyes, in the dwell between life and death. The film of their life had been played at hyper-speed across the screen of their mind.

If we can contemplate that our mind is a storage cabinet of everything that has happened to us so far within this lifetime, it becomes possible to comprehend and understand the concept of *Total Recall*.

Now we move further into the philosophical. Another widely held theory is that we have *multiple lives*. This theory suggests we come into each life to complete another chapter towards our ultimate destiny of life. Each time we experience and utilise more of our inherent, unique talents, our innate capabilities and desires, until all of our soul's desires are complete.

 When we bring these two possibilities together, we arrive at another critical point of empowerment. The Master Key of *Total Recall & Completion.* The first possibility, that the mind retains every experience and event in order to play it back at the moment of the death of this life. The second possibility, that we have multiple lives in order to fulfil our ultimate destiny of life. Together these two possibilities provide a philosophy which has the ability to *transform our world*!

Being open to these two possibilities, you hold within your hands a *Principle Guide* towards an amazing life. Our minds ability to replay every experience and event we have encountered within this lifetime enables our *being* to review what we have and have not crossed off the *to do list* of our deepest, core desires and destiny of life. These fundamental desires, held deep within our *being*, are our *truest* desires; they are the *Principle* desires that bring joy to our soul and fulfil our individual destiny.

This philosophy states that at the end of each life our events and experiences are reviewed on the screen of our mind, with the principle desires that remain unfulfilled being taken by our soul into our next life for completion.

Consciously or unconsciously, the incompletion of our core desire is what lead us to dissatisfaction. There is something burning within us, something that is aflame deep down inside that hankers for recognition. It screams for release, it demands fulfilment. Once we begin to *consciously* understand what our deepest desires are, once we have contemplated, digested, embraced and reconciled them, we have that *Holy Grail* towards our peace of mind.

The lasting happiness you seek can never be satisfied until the calling of your *Principle Desires* are heard, nurtured and released to blossom and explode. Through the process of examination, release and subsequent manifestation of your *Principle Desires*, your full magnificence will be realised.

So, if we can comprehend that we retain every memory we experience throughout our lifetime and understand that there is *no possibility of forgetting or removing our past*, we reach a point of *Transcendence*.

We use enormous quantities of energy trying to erase, block, suppress, destroy, work out or eradicate our past. Through *Transcendence*, we discover that this is a *totally unachievable goal.* Deletion cannot be attained. Your past will always be your past!

Now, you are in trouble. If you cannot get rid of your past surely, you're trapped. Trapped by those debilitating memories and recollections which destroy your every day. Trapped within a prison that has no door for escape, and now you realise something more. Your past will only be added to!

 Fortunately, a liberating, healthy, positive solution to this dilemma is available. This is within the incredibly powerful decision to **Accept Your Past as Fact.** Accept the *fact* that your' past has happened. Accept the *fact* that it is your' history. Accept the *fact* that the past has been your' evolution to this point.

Once your past is accepted as *fact*, your jailor, the robber of your happiness, is your captor no more!

You are now in control. Isn't that what you have always wanted? You have exposed the ghost that has haunted you for so long. *The ghost of past*, and its debilitating shroud that surrounded you, is destroyed. You have exposed the *fact* that this menacing spectre of past is just a collection of experiences and happenings to which you had tied emotional ropes and these massive emotional ropes had you tethered firmly to the harbour wall, namely, your harbour wall of *Limiting Beliefs*!

It is the *emotional connections* we make to our past experiences that hold us to the experience. On one side our mind is determined to deny their existence, whilst the other side constantly examines why the situation happened. We obsess about the possibilities which may have occurred if the experience had not happened. This cacophony of conflicting mind games conspires to drive the experience deeper and deeper into our subconscious. Unconsciously, we make the event, or events, rule our lives and determine how we function and operate in the outside world.

For example, a failed marriage may make us sceptical about other men or women. This will, unwittingly, determine our future relationship path. With this *limiting belief* in place, *no* other person can reach us; *no* one can get close. The depth of emotional attachment to the past experience dominates the present and future behaviour. It dominates how we now interact. Unconsciously, the pattern becomes established, thus, our future is determined by our past.

What past experiences could have been affecting that person encountered at work? The one who responded so vehemently, *"How dare you criticise what I have to say, you don't know how difficult it is for me to organise my kids and my life to fit in with the hours we currently do. It's alright for you. You have got your life sorted, what with your new car, your holidays abroad and your education. I have worked so hard to get to this position in the company, but you wouldn't understand that would you"*!

What had gone on in their past? At a time of stress, when the suppressive defences are weakened, what experiences had they pulled forward to make so many references and judgements? Had they a failed marriage, money problems, are they a single parent; or just jealous? What is the *self-image* surrounding their educational achievements? Only they and they alone will know what determines their *Limiting Beliefs*.

There is only one constructive thing we can do with the *past*; and that is to *learn from it*. The event or experience, seen as *a Fact*, coupled with the *tool of transcendence and understanding,* provide us with the template to cut those emotional ties. This template enables us to take from the past and transform our future.

The interpretation of our experiences and events we retain are normally taken in snap shot or point of time focus. We focus in on the specific scenario and link it to that moment. However, when we stretch this perspective, when we expand the time frame upon which we view the event, we see the landscape change, the perspective and the intensity of what happened change.

When we first look at a portrait, something draws our attention toward it. For instance, we see the title of the piece is called *The Harvest*. As we look closer at the picture it starts to capture our imagination. After our initial snapshot view, we begin to delve deeper within the overall picture. We begin to see the specifics contained within the overall artwork. We see the detail of the trees. We see that some of the birds are flying high in the sky, whilst others are on the ground, looking for grubs after the combine has moved on. Some of the farm hands are bailing whilst others stand waiting for the grain to be poured from the combines' hopper. The perplexed rabbit is investigating his new landscape. Just a short time ago the corn had stood tall, the run where he felt safe from predators is now no more, a new awareness now required.

When you evaluate your life in a much wider context, you can begin to change the intense power and the gestalt of the events that have occurred along the way. You can place them within your history and look at how they have affected your overall picture of life to this time. Many times, you will see that if a specific event had not happened then the next point of reference would not have occurred.

For example, that undesired loss of a job resulted in moving to another position with much greater prospects, improved level of pay and rewards. However, at the specific time it happened, the trauma felt by the person was devastating. When first told and faced with the need to find a new position, the whole scenario was extremely daunting. Concerned about their family, they worried deep into the night wondering how to keep up the mortgage payments, feed the family and pay the bills. However, as time passed, that position had been found. It had all worked out really well for them and their family.

But what could have been the reference point if that next move had not gone so well? That new company they joined were not good to work for. The company broke their promises, the career prospects they promised were never going to materialise.

Either of these scenarios can be viewed, or more importantly retained, in many ways. The intensity of these remembrances is dependent upon your outlook and perspective of life. You could retain the intense emotions of fear surrounding losing the job and the associated trauma felt at the time. Even though things are now OK, you could retain the fear that it may happen again. Now you remain perpetually on guard. You determine to never put yourself in the firing line again. You never want to deal with this scenario again as the scars run so deep. You determine to keep your head down, keep in line, work hard, be good and hopefully those emotions won't be felt again. The *postage stamp world* becomes your reality through the fear of the *unknown*!

Alternatively, you could resolve that, yes, this event happened, but overall *I now know* that I can come out the other side. If it occurred again *I know* it can and will be sorted. There may be some pain to get over but in the long run it's just a job. They come they go. I will work hard though I will never ignore my home life again just to satisfy the company goals; those days are over. I get one shot at this life and this experience has taught me that my family and what I really want to do with my life are far more important factors than any job'.

Here, once again, lays *choice,* the *Scales of Decision.* Was this experience positive or negative? Do not both of these polarities exist within this scenario?

So, is it necessary to *choose,* interpret or define a situation as positive or negative, good or bad, welcome or unwelcome? When we make a distinction of the event as one thing or another it is *filed* under its respective *Category.* That *file,* stored within you mind, will lay dormant until another, similar situation occurs.

When this similar event or experience occurs, we 're-act' unconsciously, in a similar way to how we did when it happened before. Remember, we had chosen to file it under its category in our storage cabinet of remembrances. The uncontrolled mind categorised the event and place it into a relevant file in the *belief* that it will be a useful weapon to *protect* us in the future.

 Life can only become true freedom when you *consciously* decide to discard the powerful, negative emotional ties that you link to the vast majority of your remembrances.

The method is to **Recall our Remembrances as Fact.** It sounds simple in the cold light of day, but to change the emotional experience into just a *Fact,* we must first *Accept* that the event has happened to us.

Your future health and wellbeing depends upon being able to recall these *Limiting Memories* or *embedded beliefs* as *Fact,* in order to diminish their powerful, all consuming, negative emotional ties. The ability to *de-emotionalise* these negative events, whilst *accepting* the occurrence, has the power to literally transform your world.

 To break an emotional tie is incredibly challenging. It has become *hard wired* through the repetitive layering of events within the mind. A method is required to begin this transition. The method is called **The Third Person.**

A distance must be created between us and the event. This *distance* enables us to look at the experience from a detached, de-emotionalised position. By viewing it as *The Third Person*, we begin to dis-empower the event. We are able to stand back, observe and see the event from a different perspective, from a different level.

As I have said, the only *constructive* thing we can do with our remembrances of the past is to *learn* from them. From this *Third Person, detached* perspective, who can view the relevant points of the event with diminished emotion. We can examine what went well and not so well, what we will accept and not accept again in our life and understand the *learning's* and *teachings* of this event. It has happened. It is *a Fact*. We now can look into it deeply, because we are looking from a detached, distanced standpoint, as though the event happened to someone else, or someone outside of you.

Through *detachment*, through *de-emotionalising* each event, we can then ask questions of a different quality. Has the event held us back or propelled us forward? How can it help or hinder us in the future? What is the *worth* of this *fact*?

Once we have considered, documented and determined what we can learn from the event, we possess an immense gift. We can gift to ourselves the ability to make a critical declaration. *"Enough is Enough!* I will invest no further in the self-analysis of this event. No more *'If Only......,* no more *why did this happen to me,* no more *re-enactment of what has gone before"*.

We take forward only the elements that can assist us. The remaining emotional entanglement is discarded like last weeks' rubbish. The event happened, *Fact*. We take the good things, *Fact*. We move forward, *Fact*. We look in the mirror and smile at what we have learnt, *Fact!*

 The direction towards a whole new world from our *Limiting Beliefs* is to; **Detach, View, Learn, Discard and Smile.**

My proposal is a simple philosophy, but incredibly hard to do, I know. The emotional bonds with your past are incredibly strong. Your mind yearns to find a conclusion to an event it can never conclude. You go over and over the event in your mind and try to rewrite an ending that has already happened! Believe me though when I say that the utilisation of this simple philosophy will release you from your past tormentors. You will never experience that same scenario again.

Future events may have similarities with what you have experienced, but now you know that if you project the emotionalised past onto your future situation *you will bring about the same conclusion*! This is your-self-fulfilling prophesy; and you are the cause!

If you are looking for something to occur, guess what, it will! We really do have this level of power, especially when the messages we send are loaded with deep emotional connections.

For example, we now know why no two people on earth are the same. So why would we retain a model that says, 'men are like this, women are like that; I bet the next one I meet will be the same as I have experienced before'! We may *hope* that this will not be the case, but sooner or later it will happen. The *other* confirms our long-held belief. They will act in accordance with the *Limiting Belief* we have retained and are unconsciously *looking for* from our past experiences.

It is critically important to realise that *you* are responsible for causing this to happen. You are looking for it and, given time, given your belief, given your thoughts and retained remembrances, you will bring about its manifestation. Without conscious control of the mind, *you* create your future from your past.

When we understand that the storage of the past is a mind game, when we recognise the often-overwhelming power of the limiting mind, when we become able to smile in the face of the controlling, intricate workings of the mind, we create the space for the superpower of our inner nature to re-enter our world. This superpower we felt as a child. We were in direct communication with it then, before our learning, events and experiences began to obscure and cloud our view.

Our guiding heart has become covered over time by layer upon layer of *knowledge*. *Knowledge* that is taught, *knowledge* that is experienced, *knowledge* that is helpful, *knowledge* that is unjust, *knowledge* that is unkind, *knowledge* that is important. All this knowledge is consumed by our mind and then this *knowledge* becomes us, blocking the natural guidance of the heart.

For the majority of people, they believe they *are* the mind. They believe that this *knowledge* is all they are; it is all they are *worth*. It is critically important to redefine this situation.

This *Mind* we call *ours* is *Just a Tool,* a part of us. It is our storage cabinet of *knowledge and information* that is retained to be *used* by us. It should be *Used* as a skill base, *Used* to aid our future, *Used* to assist us in the here and now. Once more, however, it is not us!

Unfortunately, the *knowledge* content of the mind dominates us. The mind uses logical strategy. It follows a process that, over time, becomes the only way we can operate. It creates within us a robotic state, an automation that always reacts in the same way, operating from the minds retained beliefs and reasoning methodology. Once we begin to recognise the game of the mind, the upside-down positioning of its dominance, we have again the power to *transform*.

We can *transform* the mind from our tormentor to our friend, though once again we must accept another critical *Fact.* Because of our huge collection of collated experiences, events and remembrances, we will have to go through a process of deep cleansing to realise this transformation. Before we can truly move on we have to go back and look at our past. We must learn the lessons it can teach us, and then we must break the emotional ties which ensnare us so tightly.

It is like taking charge of a large, overgrown garden. First, a fundamental decision must be taken. Do I want to take on this challenge? If the answer is yes; now where do I start? I could chop down some of the old trees and the grass but then where will I put it? Ah yes, the first priority must be to get a large skip that I can put all the rubbish in. I must clear everything that is so overgrown and entangled to allow me to once again see what is underneath.

Only when we have decided to cleanse our situation, taken all of the interwoven rubbish and weeds out of our garden, are we able to reveal the opening, the space, the silence and the *peace of mind* to rediscover our core purposes and desires for our life. Only when the garbage is removed can messages from the deepest part of us, our original writings, come back to us. Only when we have the space can we hear again the intimate callings of our heart.

However, we now have another *Fact* to face. When we again start listening to the messages of the heart, very often they do not follow the path of the logical mind!

Imagine the scenario of a new relationship. It has all the hallmarks of being potentially great. There are no apparent problems with their ex, the children appear to like you, there are no money concerns and as a couple you have lots of desires and values in common.

It's just that somewhere deep inside you have a nagging doubt that something isn't quite right. Things are not quite what they seem. You can't explain it, you can't rationalise it, but it is there, it's *just a feeling* that lurks in the background.

Early in the relationship you took a holiday with them and their two children. Everything seemed fine on the journey, a happy family, with you joining the crew on a new expedition. However, during the holiday, you saw a different side to this person of your dreams. You saw a different flavour of a person who, up until that point, had been gracious, fun and kind.

You saw that they wanted to control all proceedings of the holiday, and they lost their temper when things didn't go their way. You saw a look on their face of someone you didn't recognise, like they had something lurking deep within their *cupboard under the stairs*. However, as quickly as this outburst arose, things settled again, things start flowing, things relaxed.

In a quiet moment you reflected that what had occurred was not what you wanted in a relationship. It was something you swore you would never again accept or condone after your experiences from your previous relationship. As you mulled it through your mind you couldn't decide if what you saw was the real them or just a one off. Inside though, you *knew*; you just *knew*.

You *knew* that this was a latent issue, an issue of theirs where anger was present, an anger just simmering under the surface, just under that smile. Yet your logical mind had come into play. You rationalised that you were just at the start of the relationship, you muse and justify that perhaps you shouldn't have gone away so early in your time together, especially with the children. "We must have been mad, what else should I have expected. Of course there were going to be tensions, of course we were just getting to know each other, of course things will get better, just look at all we have going for us, what we have in common".

Two years later you separate. That fundamental issue remained. That issue always simmered just under the surface. The smiling delight was also capable of bursting forth with fury, angst and accusation when the pressure got too high.

But you were at fault too. You never discussed it. You never informed them of the impact it had upon you. You just *hoped* it would go away. You hoped they would calm down, get some counselling, that they would *see* that it upset you. This situation was the very same that you had experienced in your last relationship, and it had ended in the same way.

In my world of explanation, *Nature*, being life, being the Universe, being God, you chose the name, had provided this person, *gifted* them; with the opportunity to *change* the outcome. Nature said "here is a similar situation for you to handle, but I have added more pain this time, so that you will take extra notice. Now, what did you learn from your previous experience? That's right, now use that learning, and don't make the same mistakes again". But they chose to do exactly as they did before. They didn't deal with the situation as soon as it occurred. They didn't bring it to the other's attention. Yes, this was with a different person, but the outcome was the same. Where now does the blame for this conclusion lie?

I am not saying that every scenario that occurs like this is the green light to walk away. However, when we are once again aware, are conscious and have re-enabled our feelings and our intuition to lead us, we must *trust its messages* of what is right or wrong and *respond* to them. When we have uncovered and rediscovered our guiding heart, we re-connect to a power that literally transforms our life!

The mind *knows only what it knows*. It is masculine in definition. The heart is feminine. The heart is intuitive and is connected to the outside world. It is connected to all that is around us. It is not the isolated, limited conclusions of the individual mind. The heart has awareness that is outside of us. These heart messages are often unexplainable, as they reveal themselves as *just a feeling, an impulse*, though it is an intense feeling within the body; and we must listen.

The heart is our inner guide. The heart will guide us, yet it may be totally out of kilter with the logical mind. The logical mind is forever seeking solutions, creating conclusions and rational explanations to justify each situation. The heart goes direct to the source of decision. Yes or no, go or stay, left or right, up or down. The heart is instinctual, it is intuitive, it is natural, and most importantly; it is virtually always the right decision for us.

Suddenly, when we begin to believe and *see* through our heart, we realise how much we have been constrained by the *blindness* of the known mind, and how this blindness has stopped our truth from coming into our vision. As the fog of long held *Limiting Beliefs* clear, we see again the things we saw as a child. The moon somehow suspended in the sky, the staring blue eyes of a baby, the talking horse; the old lady giving her equally old husband a sound telling off!

Without the constant distraction of the past or the future, and with the removal of the mental traffic of our stored, debilitating, prescribed knowledge, the way comes for us to experience the here and now. The new, fresh, simple pleasures of what is happening in this very moment. The happiness and joy contained within this very second.

So, let's ask some fundamental questions. Why is it that we have become so distracted?

A huge Limiting Belief held by many people is one which purports that just a few people will be able to live the life of their dreams, the life they were meant to lead. These are the lucky ones, the chosen ones, the ones who have a head start in life. They have the money, the support structures, the education and the time to dedicate to their life's purpose.

I do believe that some people come into this life with a plan and a *knowing*. This *knowing* is not knowledge. I believe they have a *knowing* as to the *purpose* they are determined to achieve within this lifetime. Their *purpose* often reveals itself to them at a very young age.

In a recent TV documentary, the multiple gold medal winning cyclist Sir Chris Hoy described how, 'the fulfilling of your purpose is through hard work, dedication and the finding of what *fits* you, whilst stretching yourself to fulfil your destiny'.

He described the *fit* in athletic terms as being able to find a sport that suits your body type, your shape and your' personal capability. For example, a one hundred metre sprinter does not have the physique of a marathon runner. One build is hugely powerful, explosive over a short distance, the other lean and light to cover vast distances.

In the documentary, Chris Hoy described the sacrifices his parents made to enable him to achieve his desire for the cycling track. Every weekend was dedicated to his pursuit. From the age of seven the family would pack the car on a Friday evening after school, make a bed for the young Chris in the back, then drive 400 miles to the destination of the cycle event in which Chris would participate over the weekend.

They would travel overnight so that Chris could get his sleep and arrive at the event early in the morning. Chris would then take the opportunity to practice on the course before any of his rivals had arrived, whilst his father caught up on his sleep from the overnight drive. Chris would compete on Saturday and Sunday, the family travelling home on Sunday night, all timed perfectly to get Chris back to school for Monday morning!

As Chris reached another level of competence and success, his parents had to reach to another level too. They funded the latest model of bike to enable him to follow his dream. His family did not appear to be wealthy. They were as completely committed to their sons cause as he.

Chris spoke about the dedication and sacrifice required to reach the upper echelons of any pursuit; be it in sport, the arts, business or inner exploration. He is undoubtedly correct, but for a seemingly *lucky few* it does appear that their opportunities have been enabled by circumstances they are born into.

Bono of U2 was born the son of an opera singer. His mother died when he was fourteen and he says that this traumatic event opened his heart and inspired him to speak his words through song. When Richard Branson was four his mother made him find his own way home from a place where he had no idea of where he was. She challenged him from the earliest opportunity. Art Garfunkel at the age of five, without any training of his voice, says that he *knew* he would always be a singer. David Beckham said, "At school the teachers would ask, 'what do you want to do when you're older?' I'd say, 'I want to be a footballer.' They would say, 'No, what do you want to do, for your 'real' job?' 'I want to be a footballer', that's the only thing I ever want to do". People who met Jimi Hendrix often commented *'he 'knows' something, he's been here before'*!

Within these stories there is a common link. It's as though they knew completely who they were. They were centred, they knew where they were going, and they didn't need the *guidance* of anyone else on this earth to *know* what they wanted to do.

One of my children died when he was two and a half. Until the age of 16 months he was just a typical boy; growing normally and always so happy. One day at work I received a call from my wife, "nothing to worry about, but he's fallen down the bottom stair and he just went all floppy. He seems fine now, just thought I would let you know". Little did we know that this small, seemingly *insignificant event*; was the first sign of his life shortening illness.

For the next year we spent huge amounts of time with him in hospital, seeking to determine the diagnosis of his illness which proved to be extremely rare.

One thing, however, always struck anyone who came into my son's presence. Even though his condition caused him massive pain, together with treatments that were often invasive and traumatic, he was amazingly happy.

Some 20 years after he passed away, I found myself pondering, as I had done on so many occasions before, as to why this *event* had happened to us. What had we done to deserve it? We were nice, decent people, no problem to anyone, just normal people trying to make a life for ourselves, so why us? What could we have possibly done to deserve such pain?

Something that day suddenly struck me. Remember this was 20 years later, 20 years of seeking for an *answer*, searching for a reason that I could find some comfort within. It struck me that it wasn't about me or us, it was about him. I felt a revelation which said that he was completing something for himself. There was something still outstanding on his *to do* list; and he was with us to complete it.

As I let this revelation sit with me over the next days and weeks it never changed. There was something about it that felt complete. It felt like a *truth*, though a *truth* I could not prove. I had no way to logically explain to anyone, or myself, that I was correct, but it felt that way. We were there to help him complete something within his destiny. We were his support structure, we were his carers, we were there to give him the opportunity to complete what he needed to complete.

I have no idea what this completion was for him. What I do know is my revelation that day gave me such a feeling of peace. He will always be part of me, part of my family's history and a part of everyone who met him. His happiness was totally out of accord with the condition he suffered. I can only conclude that he *knew something* far and above anything I knew at that time.

So perhaps it is possible that some people come into the world, into this life, with a *knowing* and a platform from where they are able to fulfil their destiny. Through their geniality they have what we might call that head start, that helping hand, a privileged set of circumstances that the rest of us could only have dreamt to have.

Yet where does this hypothesis leave the rest of us? The vast majority of us who do not appear to come from this *privileged position*. It is easy to sit on this other side of the fence and use this *privileged position* philosophy as a way to explain away our current situation.

The, *it's OK for them* rationalisation, confirming that *life* has not dealt *us* the *right* cards. We can sit back, fold our arms, turn on the TV set, mould our backsides into that sofa and announce to the world, "Hey! I am not a chosen one. That's OK, I will suffer quietly, I will minimise my expectation of this life and wait for the next bus to come along".

This is the response of the loser. This is the way of the fatalist, the naysayer. I totally believe that the *rest* of us can have much of what the so called *privileged few* have. Once we become aware of how lost we have been, when we are willing to make the effort to clean our *Wall of Self Esteem* and reveal our original writings, we can create the situations and circumstances to fulfil many of our desires and move towards our destiny.

I am willing to accept that there are people, *some lucky ones*, who come into this world *knowing* their destiny. I am, however, talking about the rest of us. The *Us* who got lost along the way. The *Us* who became distracted and forgot who we were. The *Us* whose core desires were so quickly written over by another's hand. I am talking about the *Us* who didn't have the environment to realise our inherent dreams through the encouragement of others.

If we can accept that those of *Us* who *want to* can alter the course of our lives, we reach a place called *possibility*. In this world of *possibility*, the gurus would say that anything is possible for the human being who has *a dream* and the determination to do whatever it takes to achieve it. I fully see why they would say this. In no way do they want to reduce someone's ambitions to achieve anything they desired; so why would I not say this here?

Since cleansing my *Wall of Self Esteem,* I *know* that I would love to be a performing musical artist. Since stripping away the cloak that I wore for so many years, I discovered, or more aptly, re-discovered, a feeling I had as a child. I have an innate feeling that I would be in my element, in my bliss, my dharma, singing my songs and sharing my words. I would love to be able to move people with what I have to say and how I express it.

Since this re-discovery, I have taken huge action in this direction. I have had many singing lessons, worked hard on my skill to play the guitar and have written a mass of song lyrics. Whilst in the taking of all these actions I have discovered something else; it is a discovery which is hard to reach and accept.

I have discovered that no matter how many singing lessons I have, no matter how hard I try to play that damn guitar, no matter how well I practice the opening up of my diaphragm, I feel that I will never, in this lifetime, achieve the level of excellence in this area that would satisfy me. Please note when I say to you, satisfy me!

The logical mind says to never give up, continue to push and strive; challenge that statement that you will never get there, overcome your inabilities by making your fingers bleed on those strings. It will all pay off; you must keep reaching for the stars. Through the logical mind and the Dream Purveyors, we are instructed to strive to achieve that level of competence. By determination and shear hard work anyone can do anything.

I believe from a technical point of view that might be true, but from a natural, innate purity perspective I cannot delude myself. My natural, essential ability in this lifetime to be a performing musical artist is not there.

The person who is not a natural mathematician is *encouraged* to become one. The person who does not have a natural ear for languages has to try and try and try to become that linguist. The natural scientist must be an elite athlete, even though their body composition has no capacity for that level of physical exertion.

Through our deep conditioning, and the *worldly*, logical approach applied to the options we have, our true, unique, *natural gifts* get lost in a myriad of potential possibilities. Our *natural gifts* release within us a massive energy source as they are in direct contact with our purpose in life. They make us feel alive and energised when we participate in them. Yet these gifts can be lost, or if not totally lost, they can be *buried* by our focus on the *wrong things*. The societal, logical mind convinces us that we must be multi skilled, multi able, multifaceted; but at what cost?

When we fail to unearth and discover our natural gifts, and just as importantly, when we fail to recognise the things that are not natural to us, how can it be possible to determine what will truly fulfil our lives? How many amazing people have been lost to mankind, or more importantly, lost to themselves, by the non-recognition of their innate skills and abilities? How many amazing people have been lost without being encouraged to maximise the things that they are truly magnificent at doing? How many people live a life of quiet desperation; left searching in the dark for that inner fire that will ignite passion in their life?

 Through our *Limiting Beliefs* many of us fall back when we reach this point of searching. We fall through two **trap doors.** The first of these **traps doors** comes where we **Blame** our lack of progress on the doorstep of our experiences. These accumulated experiences lead us to *justified excuses.* These accumulated experiences lead us to the *blaming* of our past for our present and future.

The second *trap door* is one of **Time and Circumstance**. It is true that in some pursuits time hath no friend. The desire to be an elite athlete does embrace the physical age of the body. There is a threshold of the bodies' peak performance which cannot be ignored.

Once I had started stripping away my Limiting Beliefs; falling time and time again through those trap doors of *Blame & Time and Circumstance*, I realised how *heavy* I felt. I became aware that I was carrying *armour* to protect me from the outside world. This *armour*, this ego, I wore on a daily basis. It comprised a steel outer cover, layer upon layer of chain mail, protective woollen undergarment with foot, hand and head coverings. To the outside world virtually nothing of the *real me* was visible.

As I started to re-discover my truths, I realised that the weight of this *armour* had kept me rooted for years. As I *dressed* in the morning to shield myself, complete with the thoughts and beliefs I considered would protect me from the rigours of the world I had to navigate, I felt exhausted.

Walking out of my front door, perfectly attired with that immense shield of self-protection in place, my legs felt so heavy. This weight, this sack *of stored Limiting Beliefs*, consumed every ounce of energy I could muster. Unconsciously, I thought I could project the image I wanted to portray onto the outside world. Nothing could pierce my armour. I could control this persona I had created, and no one could see what was really going on inside, I had after all an image to protect!

I was being what I thought I should be. A businessman, a developer of people, a money generator and a *success*! To the outside world I *succeeded* to a high point, but my personal satisfaction, my health and my wellbeing were so low. I was trying to be what I thought I should be; show the outside world what I could do and become.

This path was seen by everyone around as success. I justified its attack upon my spirit and my body with the consolation that what I was doing was *right*. I must be on the *right side* of the road. I had to continue to aspire, go higher; reach further.

But every morning my legs said differently. Other than fleeting moments of happiness, that world of business gave me so little delight. It gave me money, cars, houses; but my heart was hardly alight.

In times of reflection, I realised that my rare moments of delight came from opportunities to be creative. When in an environment to build something new, create something never tried before, I had a passion for what I did. I delighted in developing people, yet continually I found in the world of business that people are used and then discarded with the same level of empathy as a paper cup.

I experienced the trauma of encouraging many peoples' efforts, helping them develop their skills and their commitment to the cause, only to see all their effort, their skill, their commitment, overlooked, discarded and ignored, when the business needs had been met. The business leaders cried, "that's just business". I just cried.

I reached a point where everything I had worked and striven for, all enclosed within that suit of armour, felt more and more wrong. The suit didn't fit me anymore. I was a creative trying to be a cold, logical, strategic businessman. I had spent many years building that *suit*, but now everything I stood for, everything I believed myself to be, everything others perceived me as, I realised wasn't the *true* me.

I knew I had to rip away all of the *Limiting Beliefs* I had created and stored and start afresh, but there was a difficulty. All of those *Limiting Beliefs* that had formed over the years had become part of me. If I now removed these beliefs, what then? Who would I be? What would I be? Would I know me? Would others know me, would they like me? What if this course of action was wrong? Where would I be then; what kind of fool would I look?

The removal of our long held *Limiting Beliefs* is a massively challenging process. These beliefs are imprinted deeply within our mind. They form the way we view the world and react to every situation.

Now you are to consciously embark on changing that view of the world. You are essentially going to change what you see from the *known* to the *unknown*. *The known* is either what we have learnt from others or what we have previously experienced. If we consider the *known* what can it give us? It can give us a *perception of comfort* as we have stood upon this ground before. It can give us a degree of control. It can provide familiarity. *We can take comfort in the belief that we know* the outcome. We *know* that if every time we react in the same way we will get a fixed result. This is a correct assumption. We can manage our *known* world in accordance with this *known* methodology which eliminates or minimises our exposure to the risk of the *unknown*.

We travel the same route to and from work each day, though we are aware of alternative routes. Our deduction is that we *know* our route always takes us 55 minutes to complete. We *know* where the jams occur, and we *know* the speed limit camera locations. *The other routes are less predictable. They can be much quicker to complete, but we never know*. We could meet a restriction behind a tractor. We have heard that sometimes there is a mobile police camera hidden from view, or there might be new pot holes we need to avoid.

The problem is that none of these *unknowns* are constants; they are *what ifs*. To take one of these *what ifs* routes requires our total presence and awareness. We have always chosen the *known* route, the constant route, the route that can be controlled as *the safe route*. The route we can travel on autopilot.

The taking of a *what if* route requires us to ignite our consciousness, our presence and our awareness. The outcome is no longer predictable, yet there is also adventure and a possibility that we can arrive far earlier than before.

Time passes through a different dimension when we are consciously in the moment. Time changes when we are consciously aware that we must respond specifically and immediately to the intense situation which presents itself through the route of the *unknown*. The *unknown* journey is fresh, alive, dynamic, and forever new. Not now the boredom of routine, not now the repetition of that same old journey day in and day out, not now the same predictable outcome.

Yet to break the stupor, the boredom, the autopilot of the *known*, takes real courage. You will not *know* what is going to happen. This alternative route may be risky; it has the possibility of danger.

As you peel away the *Limiting Beliefs* that have determined your path to this point, another critical piece of awareness must be understood. *No current belief should be replaced with another belief. You will expose beliefs that have been responsible for your behaviours, your reactions and your outcomes* to this point. These *Limiting Beliefs* have kept you anchored to the shore.

To move forward you need your *Wall of Self Esteem* to be as blank as possible. You want only to retain the bricks that describe your core desires and destiny, your unique abilities, your beneficial skills and the elements that keep you safe from physical danger.

Imagine now that you are reviewing all of the inscriptions currently written upon your wall. How many are *learnt beliefs*? How many of these beliefs *limit* you, pull you under the water, keep you anchored to where you currently are? How many are retained, *negative experiences*? How many restrict your future, making you grip hard to the *known*, to the status quo?

One by one review them. Are they positive, negative or destructive? If they are negative or destructive in any way we now have the consciousness to begin to transcend them. The model for *Belief Transformation* is; *Detach, View, Learn, Discard, and Smile.*

The exposure of your *Limiting Beliefs*, understanding and *smiling* at their hidden power, creates for you the opportunity to crush their debilitating powers. Remember, these *Limiting Beliefs* are the beliefs you hold onto that stop you from revealing your deepest core desires and destiny.

Now you are beginning to have awareness. Awareness of how these *Limiting Beliefs* have stood in your way. You must now have the bravery to bring them to the forefront of your mind. You need to be courageous and expose these demons that you have hidden; or tried to hide, from the outside world. You now need to take the bravest step of them all; *to deal with them*!

Another critical understanding now enters from stage right. When you empty the mind's storage cabinet of *limiting beliefs*, when you invest huge amounts of effort in its cleansing, what content should refill the shelves inside? Surely those empty shelves must be replenished with other, more suitable content?

When you work so hard to eradicate your *Limiting Beliefs* to expose those true writings on your *Wall of Self Esteem*; why, oh why, should you replace those old beliefs with new, different beliefs? Didn't those old beliefs dramatically get in your way? Didn't they stop you from living the life you were intended to live? Didn't they keep pulling you back in order for you to attend to them, defend them; portray them as your truth?

To *Resurrect & RECLAIM The True you,* you need to have a canvas that is as clean as possible, without a set of learnt *Limiting Beliefs*.

Even if these new beliefs are better, perhaps more positive, encouraging or more engaging, if you embed these new beliefs you will again start to operate and react from their prescription. They will now become your new way of being, your way of acting. They will again be what you stand for and protect.

To be truly open to every possibility that unfolds before you, to be no longer at the mercy of restrictions from your past, you should have, in theoretical terms, no 'set' beliefs. You operate in accordance with your feelings at that specific moment in time.

The liberation of responding to your feelings is immense. Often these feelings are seen as not *socially* the thing to do. 'You have spent your money on this film and you must see it through,' says the logical mind. But your inner guide, your natural being determined that, 'I am not enjoying this, I'm off'!

You will not now react as before through a predestined consistency. You will respond to each situation in its freshness. Today it is right, tomorrow perhaps not. You will be alive to each moment anew. You will be spontaneous to each new situation, to each new opportunity.

People will not know you as before. Before they believed they *knew you*, they *knew how you would react*, how you would *behave and respond* in any given situation. Now you are a new person; or rather, you are the person you were before your past replaced those bricks within your *Wall of Self Esteem*.

Once you are directing your own life you are the owner of the most powerful relationship! A whole relationship with your natural self; consisting of honesty, truth and integrity. This wholeness, once embraced, is truly transformational.

I honestly *know* that in this lifetime I will never be the singer and guitarist I desire to be. I *know* I don't have the innate gifts to be able to perform at the level that would satisfy me. I will continue to have those singing lessons, but I *know* that my excellence is not in my voice. I will strive to improve my guitar skills, to enjoy playing and open up new stimulus of sound; though I *know* inside I will never excel in this area. But what do I also *know*? What I have re-discovered?

I have re-discovered that I can write. I can write song lyrics, I can write poetry, I can write the stories of my experiences. Through my exhaustive exploration, I have realised that the musical score does not come to me. Others hear where a trumpet should sound, where a piano would be transformational to the piece. The music doesn't come to me. I accept this now. Rather than being envious of others' skills and hearing those haunting, debilitating thoughts of *'If Only'*.... I accept that this is not my centre of excellence.

My words are my skill, my calling, my bliss. When I write a song lyric or poem, when I am able to portray a situation I have experienced through my words, I adore it. The beauty of the lyric or poetry is in how the structure is often not grammatically correct, but in that incorrectness the magic lies. Therein lays a magic that endures time. I now *know* that the closest I can get to experiencing one of my core desires is to create the songs others can sing. I can use *their* innate talents and when they sing my lyrics, they move through me.

Am I selling myself short? Am I just giving up on a dream because I cannot reach the standard I have set for myself? Have I become lazy? Am I not willing to put the effort in? Have I reached the point where I have tried and tried and tried, but because I haven't succeeded I have thrown the towel in?

After years of striving, of trying, of experiencing the feelings of frustration, I have reached a realisation that, in this lifetime, my writing and my words are where my purpose lies. I have the ability to write the poetry for songs. I have tried and tried to discover the musically creative side of myself to unify with my writing. Yet through these efforts I have reached a point that I know my true purpose in this lifetime is to write.

I am at peace with this realisation. It feels right for me. This is not a compromise; it is a realisation. It is truly liberating to reach a point where I *know* I am in my dharma. I *know* I have again found my purpose in life which had been hidden beneath *those writings upon my wall.*

I also *know* another thing. You cannot realise your *True Self* until you have cleansed the *Limiting Beliefs* that have held you to this point. Think about it. How can you hope to perform at your highest level, in whatever form of life that is right for you, if you are trying to negotiate your way through a gruelling, energy sapping, dense tropical forest of an unclean mind and debilitating belief system?

When an artery to the heart becomes narrowed, 'furred up' through the passage of life, what is the solution? The artery is once again opened up. The blood is released to flow naturally in its correct volume. The internal pressure is released. The whole body is again satiated and cleansed with replenishing oxygen from the fresh blood flow. Once more the body is at ease and can perform at its optimum level.

Only you can *know* this point of discovery. It's not a thought; it is a feeling.

When setting out to identify your *Limiting Beliefs*, there is something else to observe: 'If something is easy for you, it is normally right'.

 When what you are doing has a flow to it, an ease, a grace, a positive energy, you are moving in the right direction. Once you have cleansed your *Wall of Self Esteem*, erased the writings of others and re-discovered your own writings, you must use the guiding premise of **what's easy is right,** to alter the direction of your life.

I do not believe in the philosophy that everything is, and should be, hard work. Most of us have tried that striving, punishing, energy sapping; health destructing philosophy that is constantly reported as *the way*. I believe life should be simple. Simple where, whatever you chose to do feels harmonious with your inner being. The most extraordinary feats are performed by people who are doing what is right for them. If running 43 marathons in 51 days feels the right thing for you to do, who is to say it is right or wrong? The taking of a year, 5 years, 10 years to re-discover who you truly are and to find your inner joy, who can say it is not the right thing to do?

If your choice feels harmonious with your inner and outer worlds, the direction is right. When you harmonise with your inner workings you are a sail boat being taken on its natural course. You glide effortlessly across an open sea; you take the power of the wind in your sail to propel you elegantly and seemingly effortlessly to your own horizon and land of discovery.

Life is a road towards truth, but the first turning must be the question; what is *truth* for you? For any of this to be truly beneficial, you must first look inside and discover the suit that will fit you perfectly on the inside, and the outside.

You can purchase a suit from the most regarded designer, but if the suit does not reflect the wearer, the *true being* inside, the suit and the wearer will have no elegance, no grace, no style; no harmony. No matter how expensive the suit, the wearer and suit will remain as two.

When you are *steering from the inside* you harmoniously direct your life towards what you want to achieve, and towards what will satisfy your inner calling. At this point of awareness, you will see the games that have been played, and comprehend how you have betrayed your own nature. You will also discover how life has kept giving you many opportunities to change your course. Once again, you return to a point of choice.

You can choose to move forward, investigate your fundamental *Limiting Beliefs*, reveal *their worth, their learning, their restrictions* and consequentially deal with them. You can choose to totally clean your *Wall of Self Esteem* and take the actions required to realise the wonders that will unfold.

You are also free to decide on another course. You now have *awareness*. You now understanding why you have reached this point, yet you may decide that you are not prepared to proceed to rediscover your truth.

You may decide you are not willing to do the work, encounter the pain, reveal your truth or embark upon a crusade to an *unknown* destination. You may decide that the writing on that *Wall* is now you. The writing is what you are, who you are. You may decide too much time has passed; it's too late to change now, perhaps next time.

The choice is yours. It is your decision, it is your life; this is your personal freedom.

Limiting Beliefs

Personal Review

- When have you reacted from your *Volcano of Past*? Can you identify what it was connected to?

- How do you feel about the possibility that the mind is a storage cabinet of everything we encounter during our lives to recall at the appropriate time, and that we may have multiple lives?

- Have you been trying to suppress, eradicate, destroy or simply 'forget' things from your past? What has been the impact upon you, your health and your progress because of these actions?

- What feelings arise when you try to accept your past? How would it feel to have *Total Recall and Completion* of the things that *Limit* your future? Are you able to see **Your Past as *FACT*?**

- When you detach from an event in your past, when you look at it from the *Third Person*, can you feel the intensity of your connection to the event change? What do you learn from this?

- What *Justified Excuses* and *time and circumstances* beliefs have you been holding onto? How correct are they? What patterns of thinking can you detect that hold you to these?

- List all of your *Limiting Beliefs*, those things that you feel hold you back, and then rank them in *order of intensity*.

- Take one of your most prominent *Limiting Beliefs* and apply the model of *Detach, View, Learn, Discard, and Smile*. What is the result? What do you learn?

- Take your next most dominant Limiting Belief and perform the same exercise. Again, what do you learn? Can you see a link with your most dominant Belief?

- Examine in the same way your top 5 Limiting Beliefs

- For you, what do you do easily? When others say, 'I couldn't have done that' when it feels like no effort to you, what were you doing? What does *What's Easy is Right* mean to you?

Remember, this is all good. You are here for a reason.

You have the potential to live the life you were born to lead

Chapter 5   *Actions*

The artists brush rests in your hand, you can paint what you like the canvas will understand

The hardest thing is to say no to those whose love you would love to know

Though if it's not their way will you wait for the shortest or longest day

"I can't cook. I never have been able to. I burn everything. I never get the order right in which to put things on. My mum never let me do anything in the kitchen. She said I would create a mess. It does annoy me now because I can never invite anyone around for a meal because I *know* it won't go right. 'If Only' my mum had shown me something. However, when I think about it, she was never happy cooking herself. Everything she cooked was really basic, and she always saw it as a task. It's just not what my family does I guess. Shame though, but that's how it is".

You are stood facing your Volcano of Past. All your accumulated *limiting beliefs* stand before you within this burning inferno. All your past experiences and events are stored within that smouldering mass. Just like the person at work scenario, you have stored all your life's challenges, traumas, dramas and learning's inside a Volcano; a Volcano named; you!

Everything you stand for, believe in, connect with, associate to, sits within this accumulated structure. As you walk you carry that heavy load with you. It's not necessarily obvious from the outside, but it's there all the same. You are the accumulated pieces of your past and oh, what a past! No one would believe what has happened to you over the years! They had to be there to believe it you cry, but you were there, and my, what a story you have to tell! And just like the tip of your finger, it is a story unique to the individual teller.

This story now however needs to be re-written. With awareness to and of your *Limiting Beliefs,* you are now charged with the *responsibility to act* upon this store of *Limitations*.

So why haven't you taken these steps before? Why haven't you taken the actions that you intuitively have known you needed to take? What has stopped you from moving forward from the constriction of Beliefs that so Limit your world? In the previous chapter I asked you to identify some of your *Limiting Beliefs*. These beliefs you will have known for many years, though probably you had feared to place them on a piece of paper. Often, through this denial, there is huge resistance or un-clarity surrounding these restrictions of our lives.

Every decision or action you want, or need to take, travels through the stored contents of your memory, your metaphoric *Volcano of Past*. Every decision or action travels through all of your accumulated *remembrances*, *Limiting Beliefs* and *conditioning* before they can reach a point of release.

 Whilst travelling through this Volcano's labyrinth of stored memories, the **Action Question** you are asking comes into direct contact with everything contained inside. Therefore, the *quality* of your decision is based upon what you contain inside. The stored content of your mind denotes the script and paints the picture upon your *Action Question*.

By the time the thought has travelled through your mind, a time measured in microseconds, the quality of your decision will have been determined by the stored ingredients of your past. As your *Action Question* travels through the rocks, boulders, lava pools and steam that rage within your Volcano of Past, it becomes engulfed by everything you store inside.

Your *Action Question* is like a *stick of pure thought* that is thrust inside a spinning vessel of candyfloss sugar. As you thrust the *stick of pure thought* inside the vessel, a massive web of stranded sugar immediately responds and connects to the stick. As the vessel swirls ever faster, more and more strands, more and more mass, more and more content gathers around the *Action Question*.

That sticky ball, an amalgamation of all your past remembrances, covers the *stick of pure thought* with a dense collection of your incumbent influences, alternatives, implications and fears. This compendium of past experiences and beliefs massively influence and affect your ability to answer your *Action Question*.

When we operate unconsciously, a huge amount of energy is consumed by the *Action Question* travelling through this latent Volcano. Massive heat builds up as the *Action Question* touches each remembrance and dramatically saps your energy store. When you are shackled from making decisions by the *quality* of the content of your mind, the *heat* generated within continues to build until it reached a critical level of energy depletion.

When we reach this point, our ability to resist and suppress our demons is lost. At this point, we encounter a resultant release of pent up fire upon an unwitting world. An internal explosion externalised. This explosion often manifests in one of two ways. In one way, the direction is spewed outward, via the externalised blaming of others, visible rage, manipulation or transferred responsibility. In the other, it travels inwards, manifesting in many forms of self-harm that require massive suppression. Whether the direction is outward or inward however the outcome is the same. You remain *Powerless* and a *Victim of circumstance*.

When you ask an *Action Question* through your inhibiting Volcano of Past, less and less decisions are made, and, as importantly, the quality of the decisions you do make can be poor. Decisions based predominantly upon your past are just a re-enactment of what has gone before. As the heat inside becomes more intense, the volcano carrier starts to look for ways to *manage* the situation. At this point your world is out of control. Your accumulated past explodes into the atmosphere pouring its contents far and wide. The past dominates the future.

Through our investigations, you now know that your *self* to this point is a *self* filled with others doctrines, retained *Limiting Beliefs*, experiences and remembrances. We now recognise that we have been operating through this model, and this is how we have been *seeing* the world.

With this understanding, you arrive at the gateway to a whole new future. You reach a point where you *know* that your past must be dealt with, understood and befriended. It must be dealt with to bring a *lasting* peace to your life. But how do we do it?

Imagine again that *stick of thought* being thrust inside that spinning vessel, though now nothing from the past sticks to it. Imagine the possibility of having a thought and making a decision where the answer is not based upon past constrictions that have formed around your *stick of thought*. The answer to your *Action Question* now comes purely from what feels right for you at that precise moment in time.

A life lived in this way is spontaneous; spontaneous to the moment in which you find yourself. One minute you are walking along a street, the next a thought comes, and you get into your car and are heading to the sea. A literal wave of thought had struck as you walked that street and your soul, your consciousness, your being, felt completely drawn to the ocean.

No thought of wrong or right, no berating of self for such a *stupid thought*. You decided to follow the purity of that thought and had moved towards what felt right for you in that specific moment in time.

This is freedom. This is living with elegance. This is living in its purest form; living with no historical restrictions to hinder your progress. However, now imagine taking this decision through your Volcano of Past.

As a child you liked the seaside, but you recall that time when you got lost. You remember that you liked the sound of the sea, but you also remember being so cold that your body felt frozen and your teeth chattered so loudly after you had braved the water. Furthermore, you also add into the mix all those *other commitments* you *should* be attending to. What would *others* say if you just took off to the coast? Would they say you were losing it, going through some sort of crisis? Would they say you were behaving strangely, after all, you had never done this sort of thing before?

So, taking all of this *evidence* into account, you conclude, *that's right, people will think this action strange.* You then begin to go around the scenario again. You reason that you have the money to go; it's your money after all. Then you remember what your parents always said, *much better putting your money to practical use rather than squandering it on some folly, on some silly thought.* You reason it's probably better to stay within the accepted realms of your life, the *known* you, as you don't want to expose yourself to the risk of others thinking that you had finally succumbed to your madness.

Decisions made through our Volcano of Past, the cess pit that is often our history, destroys the juice of spontaneity and the quality of life we deserve.

So often we are afraid of what others might say, but why? If we once again remember our *Wall of Self Esteem* and its *coverings*, we realise how comprehensively we have become distracted from our *True Self*, how distracted we are from our core desires and destiny for this lifetime. These coverings have made us hyper sensitive to the opinion of others for our *self-worth*. The replacement of our *self-belief* with the false or prescribed requirements of us by others, has removed our independence of *Action*

Question and subsequent *decision*. As we don't know who we really are anymore, the *outside* world has become our decision maker.

As you rediscover yourself, different challenges will arise. *People* who knew your *old self*, or more succinctly, your old, social self, may find this *new you* in front as a threat to *their own* belief systems. They *had you where they knew you*. They could put a label on you, they could categorise you as a person who was *defined and understood*.

Consciously or subconsciously, people who believe they have us *defined and understood* perceive that they are *above* us, and their *parental image* is at stake. They believe they are the ones in charge. Even when we become twenty, thirty fifty, seventy years of experiences, they still believe *they know best*.

These *others* can be vicious in their use of *conditional love* or fear. Many of these *others* have no idea who they are themselves. They are suffering from their own personal degree of denial, their own *Volcano of Past*. However, through you, they can feel they have a channel, an outlet, a way to manage and distract their own inner carnage, distracted into one who was sensitive to their ways.

In a hopefully unconscious way, they create for themselves a kingdom where they feel they can *lord it* over dependant people, people who they can control and rule. *Their* subservient people become *their* subjects and property. These subjects are not expected to challenge the *others* frailties or question their sensitive ego. The only requirement of their *subject* is to follow loyally their every command.

Knowingly or not, they crush the subjects self-esteem. They remove their ability to function without their very command. Should they step out of line, challenge their authority, question if something is right or wrong, they use the threat of the withdrawal of their *love* or *support*. From an early age, this threat, or actual withdrawal of love or support, traumatises the individual. The *child* may be 43, but the power and strength of this emotional weaponry results in the *other* achieving their desired intention.

These *others* do not like to be challenged. They know that just behind their facade, their face of *authority*, lays a void so deep no one could survive its depth. They know so little, but what little they believe they do know they will defend and protect by any means possible. The parent's weapon to the child is *conditional love*. The employer's weapon to the employee is *loss of income*. The countries weapon to the subject is *fight or a traitor you will be*.

The people and institutions we are lead to believe are our saviours and protectors are often so weak that they become the bully in the playground. For the individual who has low levels of *self-esteem*, it is a playground from which they can't escape, even when the end of school bell sounds. The *Self* of these authority figures is so weak, yet they use their emotional or hierarchical power to keep us even weaker. They use their pen to write all over our *Wall of Self Esteem*, until we enter their desired condition of *submission and control*.

To *Resurrect & RECLAIM The True You*, you must be fully aware of these potentially massive challenges that may confront you. The responses of *others* to your new way of being may trigger within them deeply held beliefs and fears, and you have to be ready for them!

However, the key is not to fight with them. You need to understand them and how *you* are evolving. Your way of being has been *you* for so long that your past can be triggered at the merest suggestion or sideways glance. You must prepare yourself that once you start to destroy your *Destructive Foundational Rocks*, the *Rocks* at the epicentre of your *Volcano of Past*, the responses of others could be hostile and unsupportive.

 So, what are these **Destructive Foundational Rocks** that I describe? These are the *Central Rocks* which have formed and solidified inside of you over many years, moulding, forming, festering and consequently magnifying in composition. These are the *core issues* that you have tried so hard to ignore, control, escape and distract yourself from for many years. These are your first conquest to face.

These *Destructive Foundational Rocks* are the powerhouse boulders that have held you down for so long and sit right at the base of your *Volcano of Past*. Their enormous power requires you to continually swim upstream and use massive amounts of energy just to avert disaster. These rocks are tied to your feet and continually drag you to the bottom of the river.

However, before we deal with these powerhouse boulders, before we take the steps that I am about to reveal, I need to raise your awareness to some potential possibilities.

In today's world of technology, should we want to drive to a place we have never been before we turn on our satellite navigation system, enter the address and just follow its instructions until we reach our desired destination. We may have no concept of where the destination is, but we trust in this man-made device to guide us towards a safe arrival.

When you start to *Resurrect & RECLAIM The True You*, it is not possible to follow a piece of technology. We cannot even use a well-worn map. That old map, our mind, has got us to this destination; and we have decided that this is not the destination we want to be. The challenge that lies ahead is acute and challenging. There is no definite or definitive road map to follow. A guiding hand can be given, a light shone in the right direction, but the route you will follow will be as individual as the individual walking the pathway.

When you focus upon these *Destructive Foundational Rocks* you may shake with fear. You will feel a cacophony of immense emotions. These emotions may fill you with destructive thoughts towards the face or defined experience that is ingrained upon the surface of that *Foundational Rock*.

For so long you have held these emotions in check. You have forced them down deep inside your *Volcano of Past*. You never again wanted to see that face, or recognise that experience or feel its power but now, from the very depths of your memory, I want you to allow this invader, this tyrant, this tormentor, to rise again to the surface!

We are looking for your *Primary Rocks*. These are the *Rocks* from which all other *expressions* of your volcano emanate. Like the primary colours, you most likely have 2 or 3 *Primary Rocks*. You can probably list many items to consider, but search for those painted yellow, blue or red.

These central issues impact upon and colour every other issue you carry. When these fundamental drivers of your unhappiness and distraction are identified and exposed, the beginning of your transformation is at hand. I perceive right now upon reading this, one of your *Primary Rocks* has risen to the surface, hold that thought!

When we gaze into the eyes of one of our deepest tormentors, it is easy to fall into the trap of our unconscious patterns. It is *easy* to vent at them and it is *easy* to blame *them* for where we are. These are our normal, deeply embedded responses for dealing with this situation.

A way to start to shift this situation, change the gestalt, is to move to the other polarity. If we have always repressed then we can *consciously* attack. If we have always attacked then we consciously hold back. These are the definitions for *fight or flight.* The associated emotion is placed in another dimension. It is *transferred* to another side of the same coin.

In the initial stages of transformation, this may be a method to allow you to experience a different feeling towards your aggressor. You can *consciously* alter your style and experience the difference in the way the *other party* responds to your new way.

However, what about past events and experiences that cannot be aligned or blamed on *another party*? What if it's something you cannot tangibly *transfer* onto something or someone else?

This *fight or flight* method of *transference* is not the long-term way to win your *personal* battle. When two armies fight each other there is normally a winner and a loser. When someone or a certain situation stands before you, you can decide to fight or flee from your aggressor. However, when dealing with something that you carry within; something that is stored within your mind, who or what is there to be fought, to where can you run?

 It's like trying to fight a shadow, see through fog, or eliminating the darkest night. *That Foundational Rock, that Primary Rock,* is often non-substantial. It cannot be fought with conventional weaponry. It is real to you but can be *seen* by no other. Here, the *boxing ring fight* is always the looser. Consider also; haven't you been fighting with this aggressor in this way for many years already? Where has it got you so far?

To enable you to befriend and resolve these *Destructive Foundational Rocks,* we utilise the method of, the *Art of Transcendence. Transcendence* is the enabler to transform these *Primary Rocks* from foe to friend.

The *Art of Transcendence* requires you to take a *Birds' Eye View* of the situation. You move yourself above what is immediately in front of you, expand the panorama, and take an alternative perspective.

When we look at our monster with the vision of a bird soaring high in the sky, our *Birds' Eye View* enables our ability to see the *total* picture before our eyes. We can view our *Fundamental Rock*, the occurrence, the trauma, not from a ground level, emotionally connected perspective, but from a detached position, as we soar high in the sky.

As an example; someone's identified *Destructive Foundational Rock* is a feeling and perception that their partner is very controlling. They feel they are constricted as tightly as a python's grip on its prey. They want to burst; they want to break free. They feel their partner makes all the decisions. They feel they follow them like a sheep. They feel their partner decides on the food they eat, where they go for holidays, when to move house, who they invite around for a meal. To keep the peace, they have always done what they were told, they stayed in line. They fundamentally feel their partner nullifies their very existence, and an all-pervading feeling engulfs them that they want to leave.

They dream of a life that is theirs, a life of freedom. They have tried to discuss the situation with their partner, told them that they are controlling and cried how much they are hurting them, yet nothing has changed. Their partner just replies, "there you go, moaning again!"

At this ground floor level of perspective, the two parties are in direct confrontation. It is a battle of two wills. They want their partner to change their behaviour to suit their needs. They are stood face to face, eye to eye, toe to toe; the fighters in the ring, waiting for the bell to sound!

They want their partner to recognise what they are doing to them and why they feel this way. They have turned this situation over in their mind seemingly thousands of times. They have asked themselves repeatedly, *why has this happened to me?*

Underlying all of this, however, is a part of them that is frightened to lose this relationship. They don't want to go down the road of being on their own. They ask themselves repeatedly questions of how to resolve this situation, but no answers come. Through the limited content of their mind and from their current frame of reference, their ground level perspective, they cannot see another way.

Now from another perspective, they use The Art of *Transcendence* and *rise above* this situation. They elevate into the air and look at the situation from that *Birds' Eye* vantage point. They broaden the panorama and take in the *event* over the full history of its tenure in their life.

Through this detachment, the emotional ties weaken significantly, and they become able to ask a completely different set of *action questions* from the safety of their own internal dialogue. They can ask *action questions* detached of fear, which are clear, less emotional and devoid of restrictions.

They ask the type of *action question* as if they were someone else, that *Third Person*. They ask questions where they are not seeking to protect their egos position. They ask questions where they seek to unearth the *full truth*. No one need know that they have ever asked this level of question. These types of questions will reveal their own central role in this particular part of the play they call *their life*!

Their *detached action questions* might sound something like:

Has my partner always been like this? Have they changed? What made them change? How were we behaving, or what were we experiencing at that time of change? Have I always been the same? Was it perhaps the case that when we first met I wanted, I needed, someone to direct my life?

Did I *want* them then to take control, show me the way, organise everything for us?

Were they perhaps another parent? Could it be that because of how I felt about myself the other had taken command? Did I move out of one world, my last relationship, still a child, into another, where I continued to be that child? Now, with my ego firmly in check, could I consider the possibility that this whole situation is because of how I felt about myself?

Could it be that because of all the *other peoples'* writings on my *Wall of Self Esteem*, I have never truly grown up, have never been independent? Have I ever had the courage to make the tough decisions? Could it be that now, now, I have finally reached a point where I don't want to be controlled anymore? Could it be that now; this *me* today, *needs* to take ownership for my own life?

Could it be that my insides are screaming at me to realise that I need to break free of this cycle? That I need to spread my wings and break my boundaries?

On the surface it looked as though the other was at fault and this person continually transferred the blame onto the other. Now, through the detached, *Birds Eye View* questions of *Transcendence,* they have answered themselves, and concluded that the other has always been the same; it is *they* who are different.

Now, rather than all those accusations, the blaming of the *other* for all of their distress, utilising the art of *Transcendence* and its subsequent revelations, they have become empowered with an understanding of their situation in a holistic, empathetic and mature way.

They have revealed that it is *they* who must grow up; it is *they* who wants more involvement in decisions; it is *they* who needs to take more responsibility for how things go.

Their partner may be able to understand where they are, now, today. They may be able to comprehend that things have changed and can see their needs. They may be open to a refreshed relationship that now requires a different framework, a different way of operating; a re-distribution of decision making that satisfies both of their needs.

They may even be *relieved of their duty*! They might be happy that the responsibility they have carried for so long, the *holding of their hand* and constantly pulling them forward, can now be shared towards a new horizon.

There is however another possibility. The other may not be able to understand. They may not be able to change and allow the dynamics within the relationship to alter to meet their needs. The way things were suited them. It fitted who they are. It satisfied their place in the world.

Once again, we return to a point of choice. However, this choice will have been reached from a far higher perspective. Their decision will be based upon a far greater depth of understanding and insight of both of their needs.

There may well be emotional disentanglement to be faced; an uncoupling of what once was, but things change. The world since you have been reading this has changed dramatically. Babies have been born, people told they have a new job; people told their company is closing, people have died. As the well-worn truth saying goes; *the only constant in life is change.*

We can try with all our individual might to stop the spinning wheel of the world, but we will fail. It will see our effort, smile at our having tried, yet it will continue to turn regardless. Our strength is great, but in the context of the power of the universe our individual power is incredibly small, though it is there still the same; our heart the connection.

Like the seasons, we are in a continual state of change. In order to fulfil the callings of our life, we need to take decisions that we *know* are right for us, decision from within our heart, at each moment in time.

Your heart and your insides are your guidance system. They are attached to this turning, ever changing, ever dynamic world. If you listen, your heart and your insides will show you the way. They will lead you towards ever opening doors, but you must have the bravery that when the hearts guidance feels right, even though your logic screams otherwise, you continue to walk through those open doors.

It must be understood, however, that no choice or action you take can be guaranteed to work, though they will always lead you somewhere, where once again another choice can be made.

Now here's the challenge. After years of inaction, the first actions you take can be the hardest. The inertia can be massive, the pondering extreme. You are unblocking a system that for so long has been devoid of movement. Over many years, barely a drop of natural, heart directed juice has gone through the pipe work of your decisions.

The head had ruled. The logistician prevailed, reason was king. The heart squashed under a *protective* mind which contained all of its past learning's, beliefs and experiences. Unless it could guarantee the outcome, the mind would not venture. It would not explore waters in which it could not touch the bottom.

Now, through releasing the guidance of the heart and your insides, allied with *Transcendence* and its *quality of action question*, you release a power far greater than your individual mind can ever be.

You pulsate; yet your new conclusions frighten you rigid! These conclusions are very often reached in an instant. They can be conclusions that stand so far away from your reasoning mind you feel you are entering a state of madness. You feel you are falling into a chasm; a chasm where you cannot see the ground below.

In the *conventional, externalised world* we are told to think things over, take our time to ponder the situation, weigh up all the pros and cons. Now, suddenly, we unleash a force that goes direct to source. Our heart intuitively *knows* what it is saying is right, though often we can't understand its language. Its conclusion sits perfectly well at our table; yet it is a table so far removed from where we used to sit. What type of animal have we unleashed from its enclosure?

With each choice and *'action'* you take, you move in a direction. It might be the *right* way according to this new guidance system, yet it feels like it is taking you in a direction where you surely must be going astray. Your mind wants everything guaranteed. It wants everything mapped out, every detail agreed, and all paperwork signed before the mission is commenced. The map of the mind is a map *known* to you; its logic is based upon a landscape that you have walked before.

Now, you have a revolutionary on your hands! There is no map, no *known* results. There's no paperwork to sign, as the paper is blank! It's just you, your intuition and the road ahead.

Dealing with your *Destructive Foundational Rocks* is the cornerstone for your future health. To look into their abyss, with nowhere to hide for safety, is frightening, but nothing can be more frightening than the non-recognition that these two or three *Foundational Rocks* are blocking your whole system. These are the central causes for the raging inferno that lies within your *Volcano of Past*.

How then do we deduce from our list of *Limiting Beliefs* which are the *Primary Rocks*? How do we distinguish which ones are the central propagators of our despair from the ones which are either smaller issues or are linked to the main drivers?

One of the best methods I have found is located behind the storage department door of our mind, labelled with the symbol, *"If Only"*!

For example; someone ponders the thought that *"If Only"* they could have had a great education, things would have been so, so different. Everything would have turned out much better.

They believe they really struggled at school. They collected constant criticism for their lack of concentration. They always delivered their homework on time, yet the work they compiled was always deemed as not good enough or not thorough enough, it constantly fell into the *could do better* category.

Their parents deduced that the comment in their annual report of *could do better* meant a lack of application, a lack of hard work and commitment. When compared to their sisters, they were deemed to be falling way behind. It was *clear* they would never get to the rest of the families' lofty position of education, and their parents felt failures by having such a poor scholar in the family.

As those school years passed, things got no better. They could find no subject to stimulate them, other than the sound of the bell at the end of the scholastic day. When they compared themselves to everyone else, even after all those years of education, they felt a complete academic failure.

The fact was they just didn't get it. They couldn't come to terms with how a person could stand in front of 30 pupils and *tell* them this, *tell* them that and then expect the pupil to believe what they were being told, just because they were hearing it from a teacher. They felt like an empty space that was decreed as having to be filled with something! In their early school days, they had questioned what they were being told. They wanted greater clarity and substance, yet all they received in return for their question was ridicule, an exasperated look and made to look foolish in front of the whole class.

As time went by things got worse. Not only were they being told these things, they then were required to recall what they had been told anytime they were asked. They had to memorise their *teachings*, regurgitate them in detail in an examination test, work under pressure with time and consequence constraints.

This pupil knew deep down inside that they learned by experiencing, by doing. They were practical, not theoretical. They took things on board when they were allowed to find the solution for themselves. They learnt through practical relevance and when they could *feel* that the answer was right for them. In fact, they embraced things when they *meant* something to them, rather than having to unquestioningly accept a fact provided by another.

Unfortunately, as everyone else appeared to *get it* in the way that it was being presented, they had built, over time, a belief system that they were not intelligent. They believed they failed in their scholastic endeavours because of a lack of cognitive ability and an inability to consume and regurgitate things when required.

As they were reaching the end of their school years the educators informed them that they needed to find *something* to enable them to earn a living. They needed to find a role that matched their *level* of capability, their *level* of comprehension, their *level* of intelligence.

Having repeatedly been *messaged*, externally and internally, over the course of time with this belief system, they now operated in accordance with how all concerned labelled and dressed them. The *work* was complete. The outside had written all over their *Wall of Self Esteem*.

Now their everyday operating system informed them that they had always been held back because of their *lack of education*. They constantly thought to themselves, and communicated to anyone who would listen, that they had to *become educated*. They needed to raise themselves to the level of others. They needed to find some way of avenging this curse that they have been carrying.

As they pondered this long held *feeling of failure*, they noticed how it had spilled into so many other areas of their life. The types of job they have always done. The company they kept. This *company* didn't really appeal to them, or stretch their mind, or make them feel good about anything in the world, but they were within the segment of society that others had positioned them into. They also felt that they never fitted in, it was like they were standing outside of the shop window looking in, everything happening inside yet they were not there; they were a voyeur not a participant.

However, if we challenge this perspective, elevate into that *Birds' Eye View*, what might we find?

Their belief system was founded upon their inability to accept something as a fact, just because someone else had said it was so. As an individual they needed to have proof that in fact that fact was a truth to them! It was a truth they could comprehend, something they could communicate about authentically, a truth that felt right.

In fact, they had been operating at a far higher level of intelligence than the so called *intelligent*. The *intelligent* had proved that they could listen; they could consume and could regurgitate what someone else had said as fact, but was this *intelligence*? Was this *their* truth? Without something being their own experience and their own comprehension, how could it be *their* truth?

From this *Birds' Eye View* perspective, they now reflected upon the achievements of the *family* they had always been compared against. As a point of *fact*, they realised that they were the only one who now owned their own house!

They realised that they were now earning more than the people they had always been compared with. Hang on a second! How has this happened?

Were their sisters not the ones who got all the good school reports, the glowing praise? Unlike both of their sisters, they were not on any medication for depression. Hang on, what is going on here?

The process so far has been to travel backwards and review their history. Now, to take things to another level, the seeker needs to look forward. The seeker needs to ponder the fact that they could now take action and go get *that great education*!

A variety of adult education is available to them, so is the time, so is the money. They can choose the topic or topics they want to take. Now, however, they must consider and Judge more *action questions*. *"How do I feel inside? Am I excited? When I think about this further education, do I have a rush of adrenalin that shouts and screams at me that this is the right direction? Do I feel that I am on the threshold of a whole new beginning? Or am I getting an overwhelming feeling that I will still be faced with the same situation?"*

They had always stood behind their *Limiting Belief* that *''If Only"* I'd had *a much better education.* Now, through the process of *Transcendence,* they have realised that this seemingly insurmountable obstacle had not stood in their way at all! This *Birds' Eye View* conclusion revealed that their situation was not really a calling to have that better education, a different *style* of teaching, it was in fact the recognition that they as an individual needed to learn and understand things in *their own way.*

They had to learn in a way that felt natural to them, a way for them that was truthful. They had revealed and identified a *truth* diametrically different from their long-held *belief.* This *''If Only"* which had held them back for all those years resided within them; and their individuality!

The key objective is to find and unearth the *root* of the problem. You need to find the *principle reason* why this belief had become such an issue. When we view the issue from a detached, *Birds' Eye View* perspective, we can concentrate, peruse, ponder, explore and ask ourselves those deep, honest, pure *action questions*, uninhibited by societal conditioning or the loss of our ego. As we delve ever deeper, the core, the root, the central reason will surface.

You must not look to blame, accuse or become engaged in finding a vent or an external direction for your issue. You are now the direction. You are now the director of your life. You are now fully armed with the gift of *Personal*

Responsibility. You are enabled to investigate, unravel and then re-direct the course you take.

During your investigative journey, you need to be sensitive to the possibility that you may come across a branch of the issue, stop there and begin to fix it. This is especially so when what you initially reveal appears to be a simple solution.

I urge you to be patient with this process. Pass through the leaves, navigate your way along the branches, travel down into the trunk and go deeply into the roots and fully explore what lies below.

By stopping at one of the branches, you may begin to alter the direction, only to find that the chosen solution takes you in yet another, unwanted direction.

For example, as that person in our example proceeded along a branch, it appeared that the taking of an adult education maths course would be the solution to the elimination of their *Core Limiting Belief*. However, because they had not gone deeply to find the central issue, the root of the problem, that maths course would in fact have taken them into further internal conflict. Until they fully understood their individual needs of *how they as an individual learns* the taking of that course could in fact reinforce their educational issue! If the course in which they enrolled was just like before; theoretical, chronological, numbers for numbers sake, the course wouldn't work. It didn't before, it would not again.

They needed to go deep, unearthing the roots, to ensure that their efforts lead them towards *their* better future. As they travelled through the complete tree, literally rooting out the issue; they uncovered what was truly going on with them! They revealed that their lack of educational competence *Limiting Belief* had not hindered them in the slightest!

They laugh out loud when they realise that for all those years they had been carrying around this massive *Limiting Belief*, only to find it sticking its tongue out at them, exclaiming, *fooled you!* All those years they had fooled themselves into believing that they were 'thick', unintelligent, incapable, incompetent, just because they didn't get *the way it was taught*.

Their face creases when they realise how their *belief* had wrapped itself so tightly upon their *candyfloss stick of thought* on every occasion. This *belief* had perpetually tortured them though it was totally unreal! They had dragged this *belief* into every activity they dealt with on a daily basis. A visit to the bank, a form to be completed, a bill to be paid, a mortgage decision, which pension scheme or life insurance to take out.

However, through the art of *Transcendence*, they had reviewed all these things. Every one of these activities they had dealt with. They had negotiated all of these topics and made great decisions. They had always paid their way and lived well, yet they were still carrying the weight of this perception. A weight that drained so much of their energy and caused such damage, just because of a misperception that they were incompetent at school. Now they can laugh, now they can smile, now they can look in the mirror and say, *what was all that about*!

 This person also realised that there was no point in putting the *blame* for this situation on someone else because, if they did, they would *stay attached* to that *blame*! The transference of blame onto someone or something else means we lose our **Power to Convert** the issue.

If you reflect upon people who you have blamed for things in the past, how long have you been waiting for them to take *their* responsibility? How long have you waited for *them* to clean this crap from your shoe? Where has it got you?

If you don't do it for yourself, you will be waiting for years! With the Power of *Transcendence* and the *Power to Convert* firmly in your hands, you can *let any debilitating belief* fall like a leaf into the river of learning, and again begin to walk tall.

Through their evaluation, by looking at one of their *'If Onlys*, this person discovered, or more importantly, uncovered, one of their *Destructive Foundational Rocks*. Now, through using the tools of *Transcendence* the cleansing can begin.

We must except however, that even with these tools, we cannot expect the belief we have carried for so long to disappear immediately. It can happen, a person can decide it is gone, and see it fly into the air, never for it to return; but most of us find it difficult to let go. The emotional strings are strong, and often our current persona is at stake.

For instance, having discovered the truth behind the lie, you may feel extremely foolish, as you now see that it was *your* interpretation of the situation that was wrong. Now, you must be aware that you might start to *protect your position*. After all, hadn't you always blamed everyone else for this situation? Hadn't you communicated to everyone who would listen how your current situation was because of your past? Might you look totally foolish to everyone around? Foolish in that the answer simply lay within you? I told you this journey was for the brave!

Following the discovery of your *truth* you are now able to utilise the strategy of **Detach, View, Learn, Discard, Smile** for its expulsion from your system.

 In the example I have used, with their demon now exposed, they must understand that whenever they feel the triggers associated to their perceived lack of learning, intelligence or lack of progress to this point, they now must recognise the triggers and *Own It!*

Once their demon is befriended they can smile, they can laugh, as they understand how this misperception they carried for all those years had impacted upon the quality of their life, because, come on, what else can you do!

The long-held *belief* was built upon sand. That pillar of sand had been shaped and carved into what they saw as themselves. Through utilising the *Power to Convert,* this pillar of sand can be transformed to stand up like a magnificent castle of splendour as you *Resurrect & RECLAIM the True You.*

The uncovering of your *fundamental negative beliefs* is imperative. Unresolved issues with parents, sex, physical appearance, social environment, relationships, work, schooling, a house fire, an accident, divorce, can cause *scars* for life.

Often, these *scars* are not visible. However, these *scars* are etched all over our behaviours. They are ingrained and interwoven into the way we live our daily lives. The way towards health and individual fulfilment is through the recognition and exposure of what is causing our behaviour.

This, I believe, is true, authentic intelligence. I personally suffered from that feeling of educational inadequacy for years. I didn't understand why I felt so outside of the mainstream ways of the world. It is only now that I can smile; smile after crushing one of my *Destructive Foundational Rocks* through using the art of *Transcendence* and the *Power to Convert.* I can also smile, though through clenched teeth, as I now realise that the torment I experienced overall those years, I predominantly gave to myself!

At this fundamental stage, massive action is required. Our ego will often take a complete battering. We need to be prepared to go into uncharted waters. We will be sailing with Columbus; we will be re-scripting the operating manual that has governed us for so long by sailing out into the deep ocean of the *unknown*, without the safety of the shore in view.

We need to challenge many things. For example; our peer group is massively influential upon how we go about our day. To capture its prey, the Venus fly trap is aroused by the stimulation of tiny hairs which interconnect to ensnare its victim. All of the interconnected activities that surround our *Destructive Foundational Rocks* have to be exposed.

Let us consider that an individual believes that a consequential part of their *Destructive Foundational Rock* is the use of alcohol. Alcohol itself is not the core of the issue. It is the prop, the support mechanism. It is the suppressant for the pain felt deep inside. The alcohol quells and diverts the emotions, it provides a little bit of respite from what is, or are, the fundamental issues. However, a part of dealing with this central issue will be the impact of the peer group.

This individual has become established and attached to a social group with alcohol at its epicentre. It's not just their issue with the intoxicant itself; it is that their whole social structure is saturated in something they now wish to change. Not only are they trying to remove a poison from their body, but they must understand that, unwittingly, the people they are associated with have the power to continually pull them back towards their lair. They pull them towards something that they are fighting so hard to free themselves from.

It is not the fault of the peer group for this scenario. It is the person themselves who, having decided to change their course, must take complete responsibility for changing the landscape of their world.

They have to decide if they have the strength, the resolve and the commitment to move away from the stimulants they want to change. They may have to remove themselves entirely from this peer group contact. They may have to risk their ridicule, their decision to ostracize, their wrath of non-acceptance.

The uncovering of our *Destructive Foundational Rocks*, leads us towards an integrated framework for our progress. Within the composition of a tree, we see the structure for the whole, complete, human being. When all of the elements, the visible and non-visible dimensions, are integrated and operate holistically, the result is magnificence.

For example, a person has for many years had a problem with their weight. They have tried every diet plan found in the proliferation of magazines they buy on a weekly basis. They know they can lose weight each time they are on a new diet.

Every day they tiptoe onto the scales, acutely aware of the effort they have put in to get to this point, yet as they look down they see the needle has not moved. All that denial, all that effort during the last 24 hours has transpired into nothing of gain. They have been here so many times before. When they had lost weight in the past, in a fraction of the time it took to lose it, the weight reappeared. All their effort thwarted, their sacrifice proved worthless.

However, now they feel even worse. Everyone had told them *no pain, no gain*. But they had done their part, they had followed the plan to the last letter and felt that pain, yet still they are in the same place.

Have they truly found the root of their problem? Have they been cutting a branch, when all the time there was a problem far deeper? Is the weight issue the core issue? Could there be something much more fundamental, far more powerful, *hiding* at the core of their being?

Could it be that they are putting their weight struggle as their central issue, yet perhaps this weight issue is *giving* something to them? Perhaps if they had their weight under control, might it lead them to another issue, a deeper issue that they *intuitively* know they really need to deal with? All the time they are dealing with their *weight issue* their core issue, one of *self-loathing* through their past experiences, still awaits them!

Could it be that they are surrounded by others who are constantly fighting their own weight issues, and this has become their peer group? Are they *secretly sabotaging* themselves through overeating, in order to keep themselves in a certain place? Is there something they are benefitting from, perhaps other people's attention? Could the weight issue be providing a platform, a crutch, which enables them to beat themselves up about something, is it a form of self-harm? What do they fear they would *lose* if they had no weight issue?

Our psychology acts in deeply mysterious ways. We must peel away those old layers of paper on our *Wall of Self Esteem* to see if there are other, more dominant demons lurking beneath. In many instances, people lose the weight they have desired to shed for so long, only to find that they are then faced with a myriad of other issues they were consciously unaware of.

The slimming social group they have attended for so long turns on them. Their new look is not accepted or appreciated. The others in the group begin to treat them differently. They start to receive insensitive jibes, 'oh, look at you, I suppose you think you are really something now that the stones have fallen off!' 'You won't want to know us now that you can get into those skinny jeans'.

People often worry that they will lose their partner. They have heard so many times from their loved one *I love you the way you are*. Now, what will happen if they change how they look, how they appear to the outside world?

Fundamentally, they have a *knowing* that their external is a distraction from what is truly going on inside. The weight situation takes their primary attention. Without this weight issue, they know that they would have to face more powerful demons, more challenging demons, the demons that still lie within their *Volcano of Past!*

It may of course have been that their core issue, their *Foundational Rock*, was totally due to the fact that they had not yet found their holistic diet, exercise and wellbeing formula. For many of us though, the core is somewhere else. Until we explore, unearth and comprehend the fundamental drivers of our issue, we will find ourselves continually brushing leaves from our garden path. We will use up vast quantities of energy, remain intensely unhappy and unfulfilled, until we take the time to fully consider *why* the leaves are falling in such numbers, out of their season.

Exposing, Comprehending and subsequently the taking of *Action* upon the *Destructive Foundational Rocks* which affect your behaviours, your health and your quality of life; is the central piece of work to *Resurrect & RECLAIM the True You.*

They say *unrehearsed public speaking* is the number one fear of the human being. Having to stand in front of an audience, without an opportunity to fully prepare for every eventuality, is the greatest fear we carry. Death is second! We would rather die that stand up in front of an audience and speak for two minutes. What could be happening here?

Could it be that this scenario would encapsulate *all of our inner fears* within one single event? A situation where we would reveal our latent fear that we are not intelligent? Reveal our deep-seated *belief* that we have no dress sense. Reveal that we have no idea how to communicate to other people. Reveal that we have no *real* inner confidence. Reveal we are not interesting. Would this situation expose all our latent fears and inner demons, laid bare on the floor for everyone to see?

In this situation we would be as naked as the day we were born, and would have to reveal our *nothingness* to the outside world, after all these years? Years in which we have striven to portray such a perfect public persona! Of course we would rather die than take that risk!

If we can comprehend the restrictive nature of the ego, the created persona that ensnares us so strongly, we can understand the inertia source behind the taking of the *Actions* we need to take. We are being asked to take *Actions* on subjects, and a persona, that we have invested our whole life's energies creating, and defending! So many years spent *investing* in the wrong marriage, the wrong job, the maintenance of family ties, *investing* in a public persona that was never the *True You*.

Such waste, such poor decisions, such humiliation; and now we are being asked to prostrate ourselves upon the ground and reveal that we have been going in the wrong direction, and for so long! Our ego is totally challenged. Everything we have stood for to this point is under threat and then, then, our mind projects the full catastrophe of what we are contemplating!

Through the fear of revealing our full truth, the mind projects that we are on the road to ruin. Everything we have worked for, put so much effort into, will all be lost. We surely cannot reveal such a fool to the world!

But who are we trying to fool? In historical times, the Kings and Queens had *fools* within their courts. They had a court jester, a *fool* to whom they would speak and ask their view on things. Yet what place had these *fools* within the higher echelons of society? Surely society required a much higher standing of person to guide the nobility, to address their majesties? What possible reason could the leaders of nations have for listening to such simple, uneducated, ignorant *fools*?

The worth and beauty of the *fool* was contained *within* their simplicity. Their worth was contained *within* their *lack of education* and *within* their ignorance. They were not politicians. They said their words without a desire to manipulate. They spoke *their* truth straight from *their* hearts. They spoke *their* truth without *their* words being filtered and tarnished through an enclave of beliefs, learnt education and personal objectives.

Your inner *fool*, your heart, wants to talk to you. In the taking of your *Actions*, and whilst using the heart to guide you, you must come to terms with the fact that your *fool* will often make no logical sense. It speaks direct. It speaks *your* truth. When you once again *dial into* the channel tuned to your heart, the volume is so loud, so shocking, so traumatising, that you feel surely it cannot be real. In many ways it can be diametrically opposed to everything you have thought to this point.

Once you were nice, friendly; always calm. Now your heart screams at you to be wild, run free; yell at the top of your voice. It's like a completely different person crying out from your insides, revealing an individual that you don't even recognise from those old snapshot pictures being passed around.

Is that really you? Who is this monster that has picked the lock of its cage? For so long you have been behind those bars, and now you are free to roam. But where are you to go? You don't *know* this new landscape. This new horizon is something you have never seen before. Nothing is familiar, nothing is *known*.

Choice sits once again on your doorstep. You look back. You see the confines of your cage. You see the relative comfort of a *place well known*. It is a *place* where you *know* you can survive at a level where you have the basics covered. It is a *place* where you *know* where everything is situated. The people that surround you *know* you and you *know* how they function.

Bravery is required to move the massive, *Destructive Fundamental Rocks* that block the light from your new world. Do not underestimate the task ahead. The unknown is a coin with two sides. On one side is fear, on the other side, freedom. Many things within your life will alter as a consequence of the changes you make and the *Actions* you take. It is easy to talk about these changes; to philosophise about them, dream and dwell upon them. However, it takes great bravery and courage to do something about them.

Your world will never be the same again. At first you will feel that you are moving into chaos. You will not know where you are going, you can't see the edge of that cliff or the ground below. *You* are naked to these new experiences, stimuli and opportunities, but now *you* are alive! You are more alive than you have been for years. You are alive to what your life can be and alive to what *your* potential as a human being can be.

Take the first step. Tackle number one on your *Destructive Foundational Rock* list. Strip it apart and reveal what is truly going on. Keep that vision of the tree in the mind. Keep questioning, are you tackling a leaf, a branch, the trunk or the real root of the problem?

Along with the Master Key '*If Only*' method for identifying your Rocks, there is another strategy to use for defining the core of your issues.

 We have heard of Archimedes' *Eureka moment* as the water spilled over the edge of his bath. "*I've got it*" he exclaimed. It happened to me when I examined the situation regarding my son. When you hit upon the root, the core, the answer, the conclusion, it will **lastingly feel right.** It will feel like a release, and you will experience a calmness that descends upon your mind and thoughts. Let the conclusion sit for a day or two and see if it moves. If it's right, it will remain intact. Remember, this is a heart and feeling experience that you reach by *consciously using the mind*, not the other way around. If the conclusion *lastingly feels right*, you have your guide.

Actions

Personal Review

- Remember, the event or experience has happened, **Fact.** Do not get embroiled in trying to project *'If Only' this hadn't happened*, it is a **Fact**, **it did.** The only thing you can change now is your interpretation, understanding and learning related to the **Fact.** The learnings transform into **Actions** that you need to take to enable the **Fact** to go to a place where it is at peace. You now hold the **Power to Convert** your demon from foe to friend.

- Take your list of **Limiting Beliefs**, and now start them with the phrase *'If Only"* and see how it applies. Rank them in order and identify your top 2 or 3.

- Apply the Master Key model of **Transcendence. Detach, View, Learn, Discard, Smile** to your number one *'If Only"*. What do you learn? What has now changed? What patterns of thought can you identify that knit your *Limiting Beliefs* together?

- Take your **Destructive Foundational Rock** further up into that **Birds Eye View.** From this elevated perspective, what can you now see and perceive as you look at the issue from a much wider frame of reference?

- Can you see a pattern where 'if this hadn't happened, that wouldn't have happened'; patterns which intertwine all the events and experiences? What are you learning? Remember you can never make the situation un-happen. It is a **Fact** you must **Accept** in order to move forward.

- Now, take your **Destructive Foundational Rock** and map out a plan that you will take using the tools described that enables you to define the core of the issue and the relevant actions you need to take that *lastingly feels right.* How different now is your conclusion to how you used to see it and acted upon it?

- **Take the Actions!**

Remember, this is all good. You are here for a reason.

You have the potential to live the life you were born to lead

Chapter 6   *Impacts of Actions*

If I tell you I love you could I see you walk away
If I tell you I love you will my words mean what I say
If I tell you I love you what will your brown eyes share
If I tell you I love you will I still see me there

'My boots have fallen off now! I knew if I wore my best stuff to this festival it would rain, but would I listen to myself? No. No; I had to come all rigged out to impress others with my new apparel, my new way of presenting myself to the world. Now, look at me. I look like one of those new age travellers. One foot covered by a wellington, one not; mud all over the back of me, dirt in my hair, dirt on my face. Yet more reasons why I should have stayed at home like I used to'.

When we begin to take our actions, where once in-action was our byword, it is incredibly easy to lose sight of how far we have come. Being at a festival in the first place for this person was a massive stretch from where they once were. They had never ventured to anywhere like this before. A longing inside of them yearned for so long to experience a time with thousands of others, communally listening to music in the open air. Now they are there!

The human mind is insatiable, insatiable where *experience* is concerned. Once we *experience* something, it is stored in that mental filing cabinet of ours documented *known*. This experience, the experience of going to a festival is now *known* to this person but now their mind says, their ego, their self says, I want more!

Like presents at Christmas, the anticipation lies within the seeing of something hidden behind its wrapping. Excitement is felt through the fingertips as we tear at the sheets of paper which hide the surprise inside. Through the removal of that cover we unveil the treasure contained inside and experience the feelings it brings.

But after the initial euphoria is felt the excitement somehow begins to ebb away. We now *know* what was in the box; it's great, but now it is *known*. The mind, the ego, the self, immediately begins to look for the next stimulus, the next episode in the series.

It is critically important that you consciously and continuously remind yourself of the steps you have taken. You must acknowledge every movement forward that you take. Remember; the person described had never been to a festival before. When they originally thought about going, when their finger hovered over the internet *purchase ticket* button, they were physically sick. That degree of cranial trauma made their whole system react in a massively violent way. Yet they did it, they pushed that button; and now they are there!

Together with the desire to attend this festival, they were also determined to change the way they dressed. They wanted to show a different side to themselves that had been hidden for far too long. Wave after wave of delivery van had delivered to their door. They couldn't face going to the shops to try these new designs; next time perhaps, but they had proceeded by searching online for the new image that they craved.

Wave after wave of delivery van collected the returning goods that didn't meet the transformational challenge they desired, but that was OK. Finally, they found the new clothes that did have the desired effect. These acquisitions made them feel great, in tune with how they truly wanted to dress; the *Emperor's new clothes* assisted them to feel like they were starting to become their *True Self.*

As each action is taken it gets easier. You begin to have reference points through the actions you take. You become aware that your head doesn't fall off through the taking of these steps, and you begin to realise that you are growing as an individual.

You are growing in confidence and self-esteem. You are growing with the knowledge that you can take your personal responsibility, take your individual steps to understand, take control of and fundamentally destroy those *Destructive Fundamental Rocks*. Now you begin to see the outcomes! You begin to see and feel the effects and benefits. Once you were traumatised into in-action; now you start to see and feel the seeds of a new control and perspective over your world.

At this point however, it is easy to be very critical of ourselves. *Why has it taken me all this time to realise what I have been doing? Why have I been so dumb? Why didn't I see it before? Is it too late to start now?*

Criticism of old naturally flows through your mind. Be kind now. The past has gone; you cannot go back; not for one second can you go back. Wrap your arms around yourself. Rejoice in the fact that you have finally started to see a way to a new vision of how you can live your life and realise that you have the power to never again live small.

I want to remind you of a vital piece of information. 99% of people on this planet never start this journey. How lucky are you to have discovered that transformation is possible? With each step you take you enable yourself to further unblock and release those *Destructive Fundamental Rocks* that have derailed you for so long.

Imagine with me, a man who, as they uncovered their core issues, realised that, not a *Rock* but a virtual mountain that stood before him, was in the shape of how he felt about his father. Through his willingness to examine, uncover, penetrate and be open to what he *feared* he might find; he had identified the root of virtually all of his issues. The vast majority of all his *Limiting Beliefs* sat within the relationship he had had with his father; issues experienced from a child.

He revealed that someone who should have been so important, so fundamental, so much a cornerstone of his life, had in fact dramatically crushed his very being. His father undermined everything he ever did. He criticised his school results, his choice of career, his lack of obedience; fundamentally his father criticised his every breath!

As he recalled all of the *happenings*, anger swelled inside. He knew *logically* that he should respect his father. In every book and school this is what convention said. *Logically* he should have done what his father said without question. *Logically* he should have followed his guide. *Logically* his father was older, more experienced and *must know* far more than little he did.

But that *fool* inside, that heart, that inner guide, always knew that his father was wrong. The father did not know his child. Upon the floor in front of him, the father laid only a template of *his* own internal conflict; *his* own experiences; *his* own negative perspectives on life. He did not, could not, and never would, understand or *know* what was right for his child; yet still he prescribed. He never listened, he never could.

As the years passed things got no better, in fact they deteriorated. The child cowered every time the door opened, never knowing *who* would walk through the door from work. Eyes always lowered to the floor in case he received the wrath of an unsolicited glance. A dark cloud engulfed the house as the energy inside transferred from calm to terror.

In reflection, the now *adult* began to unearth a number of truths regarding his current situation. As he was growing up he remembered he had always looked for a father figure, someone to give him guidance or a feeling of unconditional love. He realised that the only time he felt happy was when his father was absent. Holidays spent without him remained as times of joy and freedom.

As a child he had been severely bullied in school. Now he felt that this had its origins from his home experience, as his self-worth had been totally stripped away and he hadn't had the courage to fight back.

As he had grown into an *adult* he still carried all this *past* with him. It affected every element of his life. He developed a *driving force* to achieve something, prove himself *worthy*, yet despite all of his self determination to *escape* from his tormentor, they were always there, lurking just around the corner.

Often, our initial feeling when faced with our tormentor, in whatever shape it transpires, is an urge to run away. Our instincts say that we must get distance from them or it; a *separation* needs to take place. However, I would like you to dwell upon that thought.

From a *logical* perspective distance is achievable. From a *logical* perspective distance equals apart, distance equals away from, out of sight, out of mind. It is correct that physical distance can separate us from the *others* ability to affect us on a continual basis, and thus minimise their *topping up* opportunities. It is also correct that physical distance can give us the *time* to come to terms with our realisations.

However, logical distance is not the complete answer. From an *emotional* perspective, distance can bring us *closer* to our tormentor than ever! You can be on the other side of the world, but your worlds are still joined. You are still carrying *their* suitcase. You can be picking up your suitcase from the airport carousel in that distant land you have escape to, only to see a bag that looks just like *theirs* following your case around the conveyor belt!

Remember the fight or flight syndrome we looked at earlier? These are natural responses to the stimulus of an *aggressor*. In many instances, I do believe that we have to place physical distance between us and the *other* who causes our issue to be stimulated. This *other* could be a person, a job, a place, in fact anything that continually stimulates the feelings we wish to remove from our world.

Also, at this point of realisation, you need *time* to *recover* yourself. You need *time* where you do not have to deal with a stimulant that can *drain* the positive moves you are trying to make. It is like having the flu yet still needing to do everything you normally do in the course of a week. The fatigue elongates your recovery. You need to *rest*, take time for yourself to aid your speed of recovery.

This person, after many years of trying to discuss their situation with their father, always to no lasting avail, decided to cut off communications. As so often precedes these huge steps, a specific occurrence happened that caused this action to take place.

He had decided to try to explain things in another way, in the form of a letter. He carefully constructed his words to try to convey what he felt, what he was seeking and how he wanted to resolve the situation.

The day came when he nervously approached his father and presented the letter with his pure intentions inscribed. The father, upon receipt, took not one look at his writings. He looked straight forward and tore the letter to shreds right in front of his child's eyes, holding an almost exultant, steely gaze.

The final performance performed. He was left with only one way to travel. If he ever wanted to find peace of mind, the universe had now ensured that enough pain was felt to force him into taking his step of last resort. Unknowingly, now in his hands, lay his chance for *Transformation*.

He had been trying to find resolution with someone who would never seek, understand or desire resolution. He had been picking at a wound that would never heal. He was forced to remove this source of emotional turmoil from his life for a period of time, perhaps for all time, whilst he sought his deepest answers.

Now he became free without the constrictions of an emotional triangle. This emotional triangle had trapped him into feeling *victimised* and *persecuted* whilst he tried to *rescue* the situation with the other party who did not desire rescue! Now he was *free* to *expose* the *reality* of his situation.

He could *look outside* and endeavour to understand why his situation had massively impacted on his life to that point.

He began to seek answers from others. He attended seminars, read books, sought people who might be able to provide answers to his *Core Destructive Foundational Rock.* He realised that everything emanated from this central issue. Everything else was a by-product, an offshoot of the core theme, but now, how to deal with it? How to create a *label* to place on the mirror that described why he felt like an unmade jigsaw puzzle? Pieces here, pieces there, but nothing joined up. He had achieved a great deal in the outside world. He knew also that he was a person of immense possibility, yet to realise this possibility he had to solve this puzzle in front of him. Once again, nature intervened!

Throughout all of this turmoil, he had continued to strive for *external success* and were working at a senior level within a major corporation. One day, following the attendance of a senior management training program, he broke down. He felt the program had exposed all of his frailties, his inabilities and his lack of internal confidence. Without the ability to be totally prepared for all eventualities he had been exposed to his dominating fear of *not being perfect; and* he finally crumbled under the strain of protecting his many faces of personality.

His fortune was twofold. He *knew* if he were to ever move forward and find peace, he had to take massive action. The second part of his fortune came through his willingness to seek help in his quest, seek someone who could provide that label for the mirror.

A famous saying states 'when the pupil is ready the teacher will be found'. For him, he found his *label* through a clinical psychologist who identified within the first meeting the epicentre of where his issue lay.

His damaging relationship with his father had left him with *no core.* His *Wall of Self Esteem* had been reduced to total rubble. His *inner child* had been left walking alone in a desert of insecurity. Fundamentally, whilst having the appearance of an adult he still operated as a child. He had no *True Self Worth,* though he had striven to compensate for this deficit by continually striving to display to the outside world that he was worthy through his external achievements. However, these external achievements could never provide the lasting internal contentment the seeker sought. His inner child had to be embraced, held, comforted and given that missing parent he had so longed for.

A reformation of his inner world was required. The method provided for this reformation was to *embrace the inner child by their adult self*. He effectively had to become his own parent, the parent that had been missing all his life. He had to provide his own guidance, his own perspectives, and his own comfort. He had to speak to himself with respect, calmness and understanding.

Whilst he sought to *embrace the inner child* and enable his opportunity to grow and mature, he had to continue to distance himself from his tormentor. He had to take full responsibility for his situation and eliminate the possibility to have to focus upon or try to resolve or blame his tormentor for his situation. In effect, his direction of focus had to change *from blame to RECLAIM.*

This shift had wider implications. His mother, who had always been supportive and nurturing, was caught in the crossfire. She understood the reason why, but she also felt the whole family dynamic move. Occasions such as birthdays and Christmas became extremely difficult. However, the *child* was beginning to grow!

As he made the shifts required and started to be his own guardian, his marriage relationship started to alter too. In later reflection, he realised that he had left the nurturing arms of his mother and had moved almost seamlessly into the arms of another nurturer. Now, as the *child* grew, he wanted to experience more control over his world. He wanted to release the inner adventurer that had always lurked inside, but this did not fit with the previous roles and responsibilities within the family unit. He wanted to do things, spread his wings, experience things through a new set of growing adult eyes.

Other people then started to enter his life who painted a different picture of the world outside. He studied numerous ways to self-improvement. He brought books, had positive thinking CDs in the car, attended those seminars and sought like-minded people. As this *new person* evolved the chasm, the changing roles within his marriage became wider, effectively leading to the inevitable.

Although he had tried to evolve the relationship alongside his own evolvement, the needs of each party became untenable. His wife had brought things to a conclusion, but they had both *known* that things were now not right. Even though they had walked at times a seriously difficult path together, with the loss of a child and significant illness and associated challenges within the family, their time together was over. Another phase of the *child's* development had begun!

Nature once again had intervened and stated, *'OK, now I know you have learnt some stuff, but to fully realise who you are you have got to walk forward on your own for a period of time!'* In effect, the child had to truly become an adult. Nowhere now to hide, no one to blame, just him and the decisions he took. Nature had thrown him against the wall with enough associated pain to make him change. However, it did very nearly break him!

At the time he could not see it, yet this was the time that he really started to rebuild his *Wall of Self Esteem*. Every decision he took replaced a brick in his wall. The more responsibility he accepted reinforced that wall with stronger reference points, stronger beliefs and tangible results. He began to see that this massive impact in his life was in fact a massive blessing. As hard as it was, he saw a new dawn, and the shifting mist revealed a powerful message. Without this pain, without this *shift* in his situation, he could never have become a fully functioning adult, one able to realise his true calling and destiny.

His relationship with his father now also changed. Through his *new set of eyes* he saw a completely different picture. He had the capacity to see that his father was extremely damaged by his own past experiences, and that he was also a *frightened child*. He now also comprehended that his father had remained immensely angry with his past, and had channelled this anger into those closest to him.

Yet another major revelation occurred. Through this depth of understanding, the seeker found he no longer looked for the *approval* of his father. He had grown; he had *transcended* the situation, and now he understood from a completely different perspective. He could never condone his father's behaviour, but now it was *in its place*. He understood that his father *would never change*; and that only by *changing himself* would he be in charge of the situation. His life became a pleasure to walk.

As he continued to peel off his layers of self-doubt, immense creativity started to surface. He wrote a journal every day of what was happening to him. He started to write songs and poems that reflected how he felt nature and the world coincided, words that seemed to appear from nowhere. He opened himself to situations that two years before he would have said were impossible for him to comprehend. He discovered the world of dance that brought pure joy to his soul and began to explore again the world of relationships.

On a daily basis he felt he was becoming the adult he always desired to be. He began to feel comfortable in his own skin. Each time he faced a new challenge he felt himself growing, adding more substance to the adult, more quality material from which to reference. At other times he felt himself on a 'snakes and ladders' game board. Two steps forward, another two and then a slide back to where he had just come from! However, he knew inside that he had to keep going.

The new people who had come into his life, gifts again from the universe, became immense support structures. He knew he couldn't do it on his own, and he had the capacity to understand this and allow these others to assist him. When such transformation is required, the cleansing of so much past, the pride of the ego has to give way to new understandings and ways of doing things.

He also realised that his learning would never finish. If he remained *open,* he would continue to grow and continue to understand more of what this amazing world has to offer. He knew now there were no limits; that life was inexhaustible, though he also knew he had to continually choose to look for these *unlimited possibilities* and walk through ever opening doors.

Knowing you as I am starting to do, you have probably sussed something out by now, that this *he* I describe is *my* own story, thus far!

As you begin to take your actions and confront your *Destructive Foundational Rocks*, the fog, I guarantee, will slowly begin to clear. You will start to realise the distance you have strayed from the *True You*, and you will reveal the impact *they* have had upon your *Wall of Self Esteem*. So many of your bricks removed, re-written and reinstalled with what *they* wanted for you. Now, as you reassert yourself, you must be prepared that *others* may not like this new you, and *they* may get angry when you don't follow what *they* had written. Manipulative *Cards* may be played. *They* may accuse you of being disloyal, head strong, cantankerous, argumentative, deceitful. They may determine that you are now *just plain hard work*!

Be strong but understanding here. When the world in which you have been living, or more succinctly, the world you have been seeing, is revealed before your eyes, you once again have conscious choice of how you wish to continue to view the horizon.

Awareness precedes choice. The quality of your choice is determined by the level of responsibility you take. Life lived through your own choices is wild, free, challenging, renewing and forever fresh.

The way in which you respond to the Impact of your *Actions* will determine how far along your authentic path you travel. If every time you find some resistance you turn back, capitulate, say *what's the use*, you restrict your growth. Again, the level of courage you show at this stage will determine the wholeness of your being. Can you walk forward, even though the wind of resistance is raging hard, forcing itself into your face, battering all the past conditioning and beliefs you have held for so many years?

Imagine yourself looking in a mirror. Will your shoulders be back, held high and proud, or will they be slumped, laden still with the weight of remorse about an opportunity lost, another chance that presented itself for you to be true to yourself? How many times do you have to hear it? How many times has fate knocked at your door without gaining access? Is this going to be just another time for you to look back and think; *'If Only'*?

It is now time to write your own inscriptions on your *Wall of Self Esteem*. No longer will that wall contain someone else's graffiti. The only words that you will see there are the ones written by you and which speak from your heart as you look at them. The words move your soul. They capture your essence. They describe *who you truly are*. These words are yours; and will forever be!

Impact of Actions

Personal Review

- Review the ***Actions*** you have taken. What have they been? What have been the results?

- How ***Big*** have your ***Actions*** been so far? How far out of your comfort zone have they taken you? How scared have they made you feel by taking them?

- Having now started to tackle your *Destructive Foundational Rocks,* how do you feel about those *'If Only'* subjects that have held you back for so long?

- How much of an ***adult*** do you feel? Your adulthood is not your age. You may be married, you may have children, you may hold a senior position in a company; it makes no difference. Be truthful with yourself. This observation will demonstrate to you the gap between your fulfilment and your current status, and it will map for you how to proceed.

- Have you experienced through this process the situation where what you thought was a massive *'If Only'* was in fact just a leaf, a branch or the trunk of your tree, and you found that the *real* issue was so much deeper within the roots? What have you learnt? How will you apply this to how you tackle your other ***Destructive Foundational Rocks***?

- What differences have you encountered in the reactions or responses of others through taking your ***Actions***? Have some people come closer to you? Have some reacted badly? Can you identify the reasons why their responses to you have changed?

- Overall, what have you learnt so far? How far away from the ***True You*** do you feel?

- Now, what is the next ***Action*** you are going to take?

Remember, this is all good. You are here for a reason.

You have the potential to live the life you were born to lead.

Chapter 7   *Mastery of Self*

Who do I see when I remember you
A deep, deep valley of soul and blue
Never knowing your thoughts though they were so crystal to you
Outside they see so little of what's on view

The dancer walking to take centre stage is the principal figure in this play called life. Their poise is palpable, their confidence cool. They are calm, self-assured, non-aggressive, silent. You can't quite determine what it is, what they do, how they are, but you know they have that *something*.

It is as though they have an invisible thread running through the core of their body. This thread runs up their spine, into their head and appears to extend directly above them. Their centre of gravity is immovable. They turn on a perfect axis; totally in control of every movement.

Great actors have the ability to create a presence, an aura that magnetises the viewer to the screen. They capture us in a web of attraction which can often produce a feeling of envy. They pull us in with their seemingly endless confidence, clarity and power. They create around them a perception of invincibility, total control and a *knowing* of their life's path; complete with how it will unfold. Oh, 'If Only' we could be them for just one day!

However, all too often we find out that many of these actors are highly complex creatures, falling apart behind the facade of the movie set. They can create a magic and persona that lasts just as long as the cameras roll; but once the lights on the set begin to dim they get *found out*, they return to the fragile creature they know exists within.

The *Mastery of Self* is not a charade. It is not a momentary state. It is not a performance to be played only when required. It is a lasting force of nature. It is a state of *Personal Mastery* that is ever present and ever with you. It is you.

"You know, whoever did this bank job must have had inside information. They knew where everything was stored, they knew how everything worked.

They knew the exact timing and detail of every element of how this place operates. So deep was their knowledge that they must have been immensely confident in themselves to take the risks they took. In fact, they must have had such a level of confidence that they needed nothing and no one else to help them plan all of this. They were able to take all of the gold they found inside and use it in the outside world".

The *Mastery of Self* is a *feeling you get* when you truly know who and what you are. You know that every action, every activity and every response you take and make is true to your inner, authentic being. The words that flow across your vocal chords are not tainted by any false beliefs, dogmas, conditioning, experiences, taught responses, past angers or manipulative structures. Your demeanour is one of being deeply loving. You are true to your core and, under no condition, will you betray yourself or any other.

Having worked through the 7 stages to *Resurrect & RECLAIM the True You*; the *Realisations, Experiences, Choices, Limiting Beliefs, Actions* and the *Impacts of those Actions*, how could you act now in a non-authentic way? What possible good would have come from all of your efforts, your dedication to rebuilding your *Wall of Self Esteem*, if you now do not live in line with the original inscriptions you have once again found written there?

It may seem strange to contemplate, but now, at this very point, you are back to a point of choice.

When you are at the early stages of uncovering the demons that have plagued you for so long, revealing the constrictions that had you held in a python's grip for so many years, you were in fact being pulled by a force that was *outside* of you. This force impacted so powerfully upon your life that it literally forced you to change course; the syndrome I describe of being *thrown against the wall of pain*.

It is said that Buddha was kept in opulent splendour throughout his life until the age of 29. He was kept away from understanding how *normal* people's lives unfolded. He was *Distracted* from how people aged, how they had to work for their living, how they dealt with illness, how they had to fight for their shelter and the basics of life.

As the son of a king he had none of these responsibilities, yet, at the age of 29, he suddenly became aware of this *other* world. He had been kept in *splendid isolation*, yet because of this *splendid isolation,* when he did become *exposed* to this other world, it created such a shock to his system that he immediately decided to go in search of his own truth. He renounced his kingdom; he renounced his wife and new born child, he renounced his inheritance and his *security*. He became a beggar on the street.

Whatever would possess someone to *give up everything*? He had everything; though he knew he had *nothing* if he did not know his own truth. This would be a truth that was unique to him, a truth that only he would know when he found it, a truth that would enable him to feel totally in tune with the world.

For 6 years he searched. He tried every discipline that came his way. He fasted, practiced silence, chanted mantras, mixed with the masses, escaped to the hills in solitude, listened to spiritual guides, listened to the politicians; practiced every aspect of yoga. He sought out every experience that could lead him to his truth.

But to where did he arrive? After 6 years of searching, seeking, desiring, practicing, following, he was finally led back to himself. He realised that *his* truth lay within himself. He had been looking *out there* for his truth whilst all the time it was *inside* of himself. This realisation was a truth that *felt* completely right for him.

Buddha communicated his explorations, his searching's and his realisations to the world around him. 2500 years later so much of what he said is still of immense value to our world today. It was a depth of understanding that had the power to transform how people saw the world, how they interrelated with humanity and how nature is the fundamental understanding.

But here's a critical fact. His teachings are *his* teachings. They are *his* understandings. They are *his* experiences. By reading his perceptions and realisations we can intellectually comprehend his messages, but unless *we* experience them they will remain just that; intellectual understandings and constructs.

The words of others cannot be ours. We can speak them, we can shout them, we can espouse them, but unless they are our personal experiences, they remain hypothesis. They will remain philosophical; they will remain devoid of the flavour of our own heart and soul.

To truly capture our truth requires us to take the ultimate responsibility. This ultimate responsibility lies within the realisation that every action we take, in every second, minute, hour and day, remains our personal responsibility. We must realise that every move we take with our life revolves around the *choices* we *consciously* take.

'*The Mastery of Self* is the realisation that we have *Total Responsibility* for our life; and that through *conscious choice* we have the power to totally transform it. When we are cleansed of our past and are *consciously aware* we become empowered with the gift to choose every interpretation of our experiences.

The true dancer flows from their axis. Their movements emanate from the centre of their being. The invisible thread running through their core connects them to the earth and culminates at a point above their head to the sky, creating such elegance of movement that is truly mesmerising. They stand tall, their posture sublime, their body held with effortless ease.

The dancer understands the principle of energy. The connection with earth and sky provides to them a limitless energy. It provides a grace and elegance so visual, so perceptible; though it is quite impossible to describe.

When I talk about *transformation, resurrection,* what do I really mean? Do I mean we become someone different, a completely different human being than before? Do I mean we take on another dimension where no one will recognise us? Or do I mean the outcome will be a cleaned-up version of who we were? The answer to this is all!

You will be a completely different person because the *You* before *You* were distracted will once again be visible for all to see. Your walk will be different. Your walk will demonstrate a confidence you enjoyed before the conditioning of life led you to believe that you had no right to hold your head high.

There is a massive difference between someone who alters their posture in an endeavour to *portray* the perception of confidence, elegance and self-composure, to the posture of one who *truly knows*. The difference is within the naturality of their walk. It is not an act, not an adopted posture, not a constructed pose. No, their walk emanates from nature; an effortless walk as pure as a cool breeze on a hot summer's day.

When you walk with authenticity it shows. You are clean, pure and as fresh as the day you were born. You have *Transformed Yourself, you have resurrected yourself.* This *transformation* is the result of your endeavours to comprehend, understand and take action upon action against the distance from your centre you had travelled. You are once again who you were always meant to be. *Transformation and Resurrection* is thus a return to your true, natural self. You have stripped those layers of conditioned beliefs, philosophies, dogmas, traditions and structures and now live life on your own authority.

When you speak your voice is pure, it is uncontaminated. Your speech is through an unobstructed flow of self-worth, self-understanding and self-confidence. Upon reaching this stage, you realise that there is something so massive again in your life that you cannot believe that you ever let it be taken from you. You realise that no matter what anyone says you know what is right and what is wrong for you. You know what you will and what you will not have in your life and, fundamentally, you know you have succeeded in your pursuit to *Resurrect & RECLAIM the True You.*

Does this inner belief, this inner confidence, mean that no matter what others say you will never be or go wrong? There are 7 billion people in this world of ours, each one seeing the world through their own set of eyes, their own conditioning, their own beliefs and their own truths. We cannot expect even one other person to see the world as we see it. Now, however, rather than try to gain their agreement or steer them towards your view of the world, your perspective, your conclusion; you have an innate intelligence that allows them their own space. Through your inner confidence, you can allow others their opportunity to explore what is right or wrong for their own individuality.

You may find that another's point of view is correct. They provide you with additional knowledge and an understanding that feels in accord with your own truth. You now can add this to your own understanding, to the way you see things, though this is an addition to your core, rather than a substitution. It is a growth not an alteration; can you see the subtle difference?

Your house is now built on totally solid foundations. It will stand for hundreds of years. You can add to it constantly, adorn it with anything that feels a rightful addition to your truth, but you know the foundations are now once again totally sound. You are capable of continual freshness, continual growth and continual evolution.

It could be said that you are now egoless. The ego is a resistant to anything that goes against its *Limiting Beliefs*. When you are complete in yourself, you can afford to allow the ego to go, say *'goodbye, thank you for all of your efforts, but now you're no longer required'*.

The energy we consume defending the ego is massive. When we are again whole, this energy can be redirected towards our continual growth and our creativity. No one can take *you* away from *you* upon reaching this point. You will care what others say, but you now have the capacity, the depth, the elegance, the confidence to be able to consider what they have to say from the perspective of your truth; and not in the defence of your ego.

Your world is once again full of discovery. You realise that you are the equal of everyone on earth. We are all one, no one above, no one below. You are meant to be this individuation, and you are proud of *who* this world has blessed you to be.

You feel a connection to others that has been absent for so, so long. You see nature through the eyes of your childhood, where a bright blue morning sky sees birds larger than the rising sun. You can hear the rain on the window with crystal clarity. A child's belly laugh brings a smile of naturalness to your once stern face. You see glory in the pure simplicity of life.

Once you see these simple blessings you will *know* that joy is constantly at your fingertips. No gleaming yacht, no bank account, no pension scheme can match the lasting pleasure of understanding the truth that no other on earth can take away from you.

However, there is an unfortunate by product to this clarity of how life really works. You begin to realise just how unhappy the general population of the world is. You become aware of how most people walk around, filled with *their* past hurts, unhelpful beliefs, conditioning and experiences which destroy their every day. You start to *see* the *cloud* that follows almost everyone.

It is frightening when you realise that there is so much despair, grief, anger, hatred, anguish and pain walking through every street and sitting in most living rooms every night. But do you want to know what the most frightening thing about this realisation is? This used to be you, and I!

We walked the street looking at the floor. We sat there at night wondering if our life would ever change. We smiled that false smile in a desperate attempt to show the world that we were *OK*; *nothing wrong here,* yet we knew we were stuck in our *postage stamp world* whilst living in *OK'sVille* ! We walked those streets and sat in our aloneness, with our insides screaming *help me someone, please*!

The journey to this point can be a long, challenging process. For me it has taken years. When I look back I have been cleansing me for the past 15 years. Man, I must have been dirty!

I knew 15 years ago that I could not continue to live with all the baggage, the inner lies, the past hurts, the pain. I knew I had to change, but change to what?

Many philosophies of transformation say only to look forward; reach for new heights; *don't look in the rear-view mirror*. These perspectives may be quite correct for our progress however, I believe, to comprehend and understand our progress, we need to look over our shoulder and look at the footprints in the sand to see from where we have travelled.

We need to review and take stock of the steps we have taken. What have been the right and wrong paths travelled, what were the great and not so great decisions we made. This constant review of our progress enables us to gain an honest picture and understanding of where we now stand.

Through reflection, through taking that *Bird's Eye View*; the breakdown of my marriage was a massive step towards my evolution. The *universe* must have felt the timing was right; I know now it *only gives us the challenge when the time is correct*. Perhaps I was *ready for it,* though at the time I felt like a child thrust onto a neon lit stage to perform without any script, without any rehearsal, and without a safety net to catch me if I fell!

The greatest step of my evolution came from one of the most traumatic things to happen to me, and there have been quite a few I can assure you! I was thrown against that *Wall*, a *Wall* designed to make me deal with and solve so many issues I had carried for years.

Upon this *Wall*, my future would be imprinted deeply. I could stand, or I could fall, it was totally my choice. Only now, through reflection, can I see that this event was my blessing; my defining time, my greatest opportunity to release the person I always wanted to be, and become the *Master of my own self.*

Life is a continuum, a continual evolution, and the person you are today is a compendium of the road you have travelled. When you look through eyes that have been cleansed, you find your *Real Self* reflected back. You are capable of consuming the environment that surrounds you. You are acutely sensitive to the outer world. You look at the world with the eyes of a child; though they are eyes without the innocence or ignorance of a child. Your vision is through the eyes of wisdom.

That's why, when you look at *others*, you can see and feel their despair. You must understand this, and, in certain ways, you have to protect yourself. You have the capacity to understand, comprehend and have compassion for their hurt, but you must retain the realisation that their hurt is not your hurt; you do not have to own their cries.

This is not a block or a suppression of what you feel, it is a realisation that you must ensure your enlightenment, your reformation, is not sabotaged by the non-understanding of others. You may well feel that there are fewer and fewer people who you can associate with. You realise when taking your actions and reviewing who you were associated with, that you become acutely aware of who can remove energy from your system. These people or situations still carry wounds of the past, and they can sap you.

So how then could we help these *others*? With all this new-found knowledge and the effort you have made, it must surely be right to spread the word? The way must be to spread the gospel, help others gain the peace of mind you have found? Through my experience I have found the best way to help *others* is to let them come to you!

During my early stages of rediscovery, I tried to preach that gospel. I would take every opportunity to tell people what I had learnt, what had worked for me, what they could do and the benefits they would find. In some cases, I'm sure my advice was useful, but in the main I now feel that I was prescribing medicine from my own world, a medicine that was only truly a remedy for *my* personal ailments. I felt better, so I wanted to help others to feel the same.

Also, through reflection, I now know that I was not ready to share what I had learnt. I had been writing out prescriptions before being fully qualified. The world of how the human mind works is so much more complex than that of the mechanical human body. A broken bone is treated in a specific way, though even these treatments evolve over time. The human mind is the most complex dimension on earth and the treatments are myriad. With such a vast array of possible solutions and alternatives to call upon, who was I to say which way was wrong, or which way was right! It was a worthy cause, though now I see things in quite a different way.

People will only change if they want to. They must want it so bad that they are willing to go through what you have, the highs the lows, the struggles, the pains, the trying of so many different things in order to change their world. They must want it to the core of their life.

Sometimes, *we* might want others to change to be what *we* want *them* to be. Our desire might be hidden, it might be wrapped in so much care it is almost imperceptible, but it is there. We want them to become *this* because they *then* will match what we want.

As I have said, the vast majority of people will never change. Whether it's fate; karma, the wrong lifetime, circumstance, it matters not. When we take the steps to change our life, when we find a new horizon which transforms our world, it saddens us when we realise that the vast majority of people will never see another way. 99.9% of people will never alter their ways towards a better life. I longed for my father to see life in a different way, he never did.

Why this is so I do not know. For someone to decide not to move forward, even when a true friend is there with a loving helping hand, is beyond me, though probably this beyond is the reason why.

Let people come to you. People will enter into your life as you go about your day. Their visit may be for a lifetime, a week, a day; it could be just one conversation, but through your enlightenment you have a *natural power* to help them on their journey, to aid their transform.

This *natural power* you now own is not learnt from a text book or lifted from a seminar. It is not an embedded, philosophical belief or something you have seen on a TV program. It has come through the transforming power of *your experience. You* have *experienced* this transformation. It is not something you have passed an examination in, it is not the regurgitation of someone else's thesis on their pet subject. It is something emanating, pulsating, bursting from your very core, and people can feel it. It is you as nature intended you to be.

At this stage you stand outside of society. You are no longer *socialised*. You see the world as it is, rather than by how anyone else wants it to be seen.

You now look at the world with fresh, unprejudiced eyes. The society has no control of you; you are now free to be completely you, and you respond to each situation in its uniqueness. You look at each situation without the stimulus of the past. You can see the games at play and you laugh in their face, metaphorically of course!

You see what they are trying to do but now you understand their strategy. You understand why you felt so bad for so long. You understand that as long as there is breath in your body their methods will never again work their spell. You stand proud, with both feet placed firmly on Terra Firma.

This is the ultimate responsibility. In the beginning this freedom feels so alien to those of us who have experienced the massive constrictions of the factors we call society. It is hard to grasp and except that we could, and have, fought our way out of its clutches and re-emerged with wisdom. This is a *Wisdom* that is far beyond the average; however, you must be aware that, to some *others*, your freedom will be a threat to them! They may assert that you are indeed positioning yourself as distinct from the crowd. This is not a positioning. It is reality.

You respond to each individual circumstance in accordance with your experience and your feelings, as opposed to the expected reactions of the society. You will not be predictable. One day you respond to a situation in one way, the next your response could be different. You respond in accordance to how you feel about the immediate situation that lies before you in that moment in time.

A good friend calls to ask your opinion on how to deal with a family member who is causing upset surrounding arrangements for a forthcoming wedding. Specifically, your friend is challenging the seating arrangements at the reception. You suggest to them that they should just accept that they are not sorting the seating plan and go with the flow, just allow the situation to unfold naturally.

The next day, you learn through another source that the person arranging the seating plan has a personal vendetta against your good friend. They had placed them, knowingly, on a 'difficult' table. Now, with this enhanced level of knowledge and understanding, you ask your friend about the situation that exists between themselves and the family member doing the planning.

They now admit that they had fallen out with them and hadn't spoken since that time. Now, through this increased level of understanding, your response may well be different. Through the increase of knowledge and fact that has been revealed to you within just a 24-hour period, what felt the right thing to say the day before may now not engender the same response.

The world as I say is a continuum. It is always dynamic, always moving, always flowing. We are constantly within this continuum of evolution. To understand this fact of life is to discover the way to stay ever fresh, ever alert and ever young.

The vast majority try to control and stop the wheel of time, or more accurately, the wheel that is the continuum. The ego wants to gather every fact, judge it, place it before the jury of its own experiences, beliefs and fixed positions, and then cast its sentence.

Meanwhile, as this ego process is in progress, the wheel has continued to turn. Whilst the jury is sent out to consider its verdict so much has changed. Nothing is where it was or how it was. So much has happened which now changes the context of the judgement the ego had reached. When we are alert to this perpetual process and continuum of time we transcend the restrictive, *postage stamp vision* of the controlling mind.

You feel that you are *witnessing* the world from afar. It's as though everything is going on around you, but you are separate, you are not involved; you are a *watcher* looking at life sat on the top of a wall. This wall, your *Wall of Self Esteem*, is now, however, your own. You own it. It is yours and no one will ever again replace a brick without your consent. When the ego is finished, when it is understood, when it is embraced, you become open to anything you may wish to write upon a new brick, and place it wherever you like into your wall.

This *witnessing*, this observational perspective, this *Bird's Eye View*, is frightening and blissful in one. Frightening because the world in which you used to function now looks totally different. You can see the games and your sensations are taken to an extreme level. You often feel overwhelmed, especially in a crowded place, as the cumulative anguish reaches a crescendo. Your heightened sensitivity enables you to feel everything that is going on around.

The bliss you feel is contained within the fact that *you can once again feel the world*. It is incredible to rediscover the vision you had as a child; though this vision is now coupled with the wisdom of your understanding.

You have reached the top of the mountain; a mountain that so few people will ever see. You didn't take the easy route to this destination. No helicopter, no cable car, no sleigh was used to ease your journey to the summit. You walked every step, and now you can see and observe the world from a completely different panorama.

But now what?   What now do you do with this *transcendence*? This *Resurrection*? You have reached a pinnacle so few people will ever see, but is this it? Do you reach this far, gain the highest-grade mark available to mankind, and then spend the rest of your life staring at your navel?

Do you just become a silent monk, shut away in the mountains spending your days chanting and burning incense sticks? You have rediscovered your freedom, you have *Resurrected & RECLAIMed the true you*, but does this freedom now mean you have to remain separate from the everyday world?

At this point a fresh challenge arises. For so many years we have desired to arrive at this destination. Free from our past, completely at one with ourselves. We understand what is right and what is wrong for us at each individual moment in time. We understand that in another moment in time what was right so shortly before could be wrong the next. We are open to all possibility, and we understand that life is a continuum, a perpetual cycle, ever moving, ever flowing. So now what?

When I reached this stage, I felt cheated. I felt I had done all of the work to transform my world from a life of anxiety, confusion, smallness and traumatisation, to a life free from all those things. I felt like a man in the truest sense of the word. I saw the world in a totally different way than before. People said I had changed completely. I had always been known as a nice guy, but now I was perceptibly different. I became more giving, more loving, open, more understanding, less controlling and totally open to possibility.

I had stood tall and had come back time and time again from a number of major impacts that life had thrown my way. With reflection, I could now see that these major events were designed to assist me with my process of Reformation. They effectively had *made* me change. I could say that I had no choice, though now I know that I did have other choices. I could have looked at these impacts and seen them as just destructive, negative, debilitating, and taken another road.

Perhaps that 'other' road was in a bottle. Perhaps that road would have led to my destruction, to a road lined with blame, spite or raging anger. But I took the decision to keep battling through. I kept coming up for air and moving on; the boxer in the other corner hit me so hard, but I took those impacts, impacts which somehow just made me stronger. Each hit gave me more understanding, more growth and more resilience. Yet, after battling through to what I thought was the end of the bout, I reached a point where I felt, *what now?*

I had *known* my purpose to that point had been to *find myself.* A rather naff, overly used definition, though the only one that fits with what I was searching for. So, here I was, I had found *me*, and my reward was? 'Come on now life' I screamed, 'I have done all of these things, I have taken so many actions, now open up those doors! Reveal to me what I am supposed to see from the top of this mountain'!

I learnt along the way that in the early stages of our search, the actions we need to take come easily. They are obvious, they are clearly defined. In essence; they are unavoidable. They speak to you with a voice so loud that you cannot fail to hear them. They sleep with you at night. They torment your day. They drain your body of energy. They have been with you for so long that they have become your constant companion, perhaps your *closest friend*!

The taking of these primary actions are what could be described *as in accord with the way society works.* They are *effort* orientated. They are in the *action* mode, the *doing* mode. There is *something* to tackle, *something* tangible to achieve, there is *something* that you can measure your progress against; a goal can be scored, a star awarded.

From those *Destructive Fundamental Rocks* to the smallest pebbles contained within my *Volcano of Past,* I had worked through them all. I deduced that I in truth had only one massive *Destructive Fundamental Rock*, being the relationship with my father, that had created every other issue contained within my Volcano. This was the absolute root of my problems. I tackled this first, and then proceeded to clear all the other significant boulders which had formed on my *tree* from this root cause. I had now reached the position for which I had been striving for so long.

I could smell the freshness of the air. I felt more alive than at any time I could remember. I walked tall and proud wherever my feet took me, and at times I experienced the magnificence of what I had been searching. But now, having reached this point, what was I supposed to do with this *new* person I could see in the mirror?

During the time of taking my unavoidable actions, I had put myself on the line in many ways; one of them being financial. I opted during this period to exist on very little money, actually, five times less than I knew I was *worth* in the commercial world. Instinctively, I knew that if I were to take this opportunity to cleanse my canvas, I needed a period of time, not of months but perhaps years, to have the independence to release the *true me*. I needed to be out of the mainstream world of business which, at the level I had been operating, consumed vast amounts of my time and energy. It also required me to concentrate on the demands of *others*; therefore, little time was left for self-reflection and personal development.

So, my *instincts told me* what I needed, but I want you now to see how life's seemingly extraneous, non-related *happenings* transpire to enable us to take a different road; if we so choose.

Three years before I experienced one of my major *thrown against the wall* happenings, the breakup of my 25-year marriage, I had started my own Management and Sales Training Company. As part of getting my business off the ground, I sometimes worked in association with another training organisation, and here I would meet someone who was to become a mentor, guide and lifelong friend.

I met someone who not only was a major player in the world of sales training but, far more importantly as it transpired, had a vision and view of the world which was aligned to mine. He, like I, saw things in a way people would very much describe as *different*.

Our backgrounds and upbringing however could not have been more dissimilar. We were seemingly from totally opposite sides of the track, but that mattered not, there was a connection. Between us there was a kindred spirit. Here was someone who *understood me*; he knew where I was coming from, though what a battle he now had on his hands!

In terms of time on planet earth, my new friend was 20 years ahead of me, though there was no gap in perceptible terms. Working and travelling together gave us time and opportunity to speak deeply about a massive range of subjects, whilst it further revealed an astonishing similarity in the composition of our experiences to date.

We were both only children, had both endured the trauma of losing children when they were very young, we were both Virgo's, we were both fitness nuts. We were also extremely independent people, who really struggled doing what others told us to do.

Link these elements with a kinship for the development and potential of the human being, and you have a pretty hot recipe.

At this early time of getting to know each other, there was one major fact that was different between us. He had been divorced. How was I to know that within a relatively short space of time this would also be another common link between us; though he foresaw its happening!

My training business provided me with the time and freedom to spend on myself. I could go *in to* Corporate Land and earn enough to come *out* again as soon as the programs were delivered. When I went *in* I felt I gave my best, thought I knew very early on that corporate life was not a life I now wanted to be in. Whether this was for the short or long term I did not know. What I did know however, was that being *out* was best for me at this stage of my growth. I needed to have an environment that gave me the freedom to be myself on a long-term basis, not an environment that only allowed me tiny opportunities to look inside.

However, after a couple of years, I reached a point where the financial challenges were starting to be too much to take. Year after year of just getting by took its toll, whilst at the same time dealing with those external messages and pressures of society! You know the ones, 'Clear your mortgage, build a pension, create money for an extraordinary social life, replace the windows'; on many, many days my decision seemed like madness, what the hell was I doing?

I now however, had this very special friend who was assisting me in the understanding of how much I had been living someone else's life. He was also a rock, as was his wife, when during this period of time my marriage broke down.

My desire to unearth what was really hidden behind all my layers had revealed an adventurer. I began to realise a person who really didn't want to adhere to societies' terms of contract. I am not an anarchist, burning cars and demonstrating at every rally. I just want to live life on my own terms, being *true* to who I am. My wife wanted a more straightforward, conventional existence; nothing wrong in that, other than if it is not correct for you.

The split of our marriage was not, however, at my insistence. The break nearly broke me at first. My friend was a constant companion throughout this period. His was a knowing, guiding hand, someone who knew what I was going through. He also knew it would be the making of me, but only the continuum of time would prove this to be a fact!

If we can comprehend the possibility that life provides us with 'things' *outside* of our actions, *powerful drivers* designed to help us change, we come to realise that operating at our best within the universe is a *co-productive* thing. Yes, we must take the actions that come through the realisations that emanate through our cognitive mind, but we need also to embrace the fact that other '*things*' happen that are gifts from another dimension.

So, behold, I was once again to be presented with another traveller to assist me on my voyage; and man, how different was this one!

After my divorce I had managed to retain the family home having considered its sale. I contemplated a fresh start; a new horizon, clear the stage and start a new performance. I contacted estate agents, paid for a sales pack, agreed a selling price and put the house on the market. But there was a problem; it felt wrong. Something deep inside me said no. I felt no elation, no excitement, no feeling of release. The whole thing just didn't feel the right thing to do.

When I looked at things from my logical mind this feeling made no sense. I could clear the mortgage, find a new place to make my own and open up a whole new world for myself. But it just felt wrong. I couldn't explain it. I couldn't put a rational explanation to my decision when I instructed the estate agent to take the *for sale* sign down. This feeling I had was so powerful, yet irrational. I knew though that I had to listen to my insides. *For now,* it appeared, I was staying put!

My home was on the end of a terrace of houses, half a mile outside of a small town. I had brilliant neighbours who had been really supportive to me through the months following my marriage breakup. I lived at number 8. Number 6 in the terrace had for some years been a rental property, with a number of tenants coming and going over those years. 18 months after my marriage split, number 6 was awaiting a new resident, and hey I thought, you never know, perhaps the new love of my life could be moving in?

Well, it certainly wasn't her! On the day of his arrival, I spoke to the individual moving his stuff into number 6, and deduced that not only did he feel like a veritable *tour de-force,* his dress sense resembled that of a tramp!

Beads in his beard like a galleon ship pirate, clothes that were assembled from different times, piercing blue eyes with the intensity of a raging inferno and a vocal delivery that made your hair stand on end after just a 5-minute conversation!

The intensity of this latest visitor to the terrace was astounding. You got 100% of his presence at every meeting! The effect of this presence upon me was a complete draining of my energy, as I desperately tried to hang on by my fingertips whilst caught in the ferocity of his delivery!

Little by little, however, we began to form an unlikely union. About a year before the arrival of *Nature Boy*, a name with which I quickly christened him, I had started to write songs and poetry. Words were being released from somewhere deep inside of me due to all the emotional turmoil I had gone through. I had an urge to put pen to paper on every occasion. During the first year of my marriage breakdown I wrote a journal every day where I expressed my emotions, exorcising them from my head to a place where I could either review them at a later time, or put them on a fire! Whatever the future purpose, I was compelled to write.

Very shortly after meeting *Nature Boy*, whilst a lull occurred from his full-scale description of how the world *really was*, he said to me *"you are a writer"*. At this point I had not shared any of my journal scribbling, songs or poems with him. I had not revealed that I had written and released a book about how to recover from a *Relationship Split*. I was still very much a corporate *bod*, a personality light years away from the raw and abrasive character that had now started to eat at my table during any lunchtime I was at home!

Yet here he was exposing something that had always been inside of me. The written word was the only subject I had received any good feedback for from school. Not writings where I just had to regurgitate what had been placed upon the blackboard, or words lifted from a chapter in an exercise book, but writings that came from my own cranial chamber.

A speller however was not me, a punctuator, no, not me also, excellent handwriting, no, not me; but a story teller, yes, now that *was* me! Yet at school, what did those teachers focus upon? My *'in-abilities'*. They ignored my natural talent; they dismissed something in which I might have future potential with their determination to ensure that my *skills* matched the requirements of the curriculum. The red rings around every piece of written work I created obliterated the quality, good or not so good, of what lay underneath. Could they not, just once, please empathise with the fact that a left-handed person, writing with ink, gets smudges on the paper!

I remember thinking at that early stage 'please read what I have written; don't just enjoy using your red pen like a dagger to my heart'. But I never said those thoughts. Like so many of us, I took the route, the direction that, *they must be right 'I am no good at this*. I don't get the spelling right, a comma and apostrophe I know go somewhere in this, and I guess I am messy when writing, just ask my mum and her endless endeavours trying to clean my shirts!

The cast however had been set. For so many years to come, something that was natural, part of my true *vocation*, was to be laid under a thick pile of criticism and discouragement. Self-doubt and a deep belief formed within me that *my calling* must be somewhere else; my *Self Belief* now matched what others were saying.

Now, so many years later, here was a newcomer to my life opening a chapter of my book that I thought had been closed so long ago. He didn't tell me what I had to do, what type of material I should write, how to go about it or where to market it. He just said, *"you are a writer"*. How did he know? What had he seen in me? What possible evidence could he be basing his theory upon?

When someone looks at you through unprejudiced eyes they see the *True You*. My new friend, *Nature Boy,* said it as he saw it. He had no agenda. He did not need to say the *right* thing. He was not trying to keep me in my place, get one over me; lead me in a wrong direction. He said what he saw. Here was someone who saw the world through untainted eyes.

Here was someone who did not take what the outside world said as gospel. He, like he did with me, could see through to the *truth*. His route to truth was direct. He did not appraise, evaluate, reflect, vacillate; he just saw it with the clarity of a laser beam.

When he said things, it felt like the very foundations of all my belief structures were destroyed in seconds. When someone cuts through things so brutally it's challenging, it's exhausting, and it's often traumatising to the recipient. Time and time again I would leave his presence feeling like the world I had lived in for all these years had been a total lie. The problem was, I knew he was right!

With this type of *educator* in your midst your ego is perpetually challenged. You begin to wonder 'what next'? What will be the next thing that I believed for so long as *right* only for it now to be challenged and viewed in a completely different way? Was there anything I knew that was right, or had I got it all wrong? Layer upon layer of conditioned learning's were being stripped away in the most challenging way possible, but was that not the point?

When things are delivered with only subtlety, with softness, made easy, made comfortable, can the message still be received in a way that is powerful enough to shock the recipient into doing something with that learning? Sometimes we need to hear that screeching car, that pounding music, that loud bang, in order to move our senses!

My new friend, *Nature Boy,* had no intention of taking it easy on me! If I wanted to know *his* truth then I would receive it in the most powerful way, and then it was up to me what I did with it.

This was an *educational process* where my previous layers of belief, which I knew intuitively were wrong, were totally stripped away.

I totally believe my two coaches were provided to me from the *outside* to assist me to become the person who could write this tale. One was a deeply insightful, elegant, process-orientated teacher who understood the operating structure and methodologies that surround the way the world works. The other was completely raw!

One coach came from the world of commerce, education and philosophy, the other came from the world of the wild. One could easily slip in and out of the commercial world whilst the other stood totally on the other extreme, disgusted at the ways of business, religion and politics.

Now in retrospect, now from that *Bird's Eye View,* I clearly see that when

I add my two coaches to my own educational endeavours, the reading of many books about other seekers, especially an Indian sage who spoke so clearly to me through his pages, I had received a culmination of *events* that were *designed* to transform this person who got lost so long ago.

Was this just fate? Had I just been lucky? Were the Gods 'shining down' on me? When I consider the challenges I had faced in my life I could argue for days how none of these could be true; but was that correct?

I believe that this is a co-created world. Whilst events, challenges and opportunities do happen to us, it is how we interpret and respond to these occurrences that makes the difference. It is in our hands. It is our responsibility to examine what occurs, it is our responsibility to understand if there is a reason for its occurrence; or if we need to just accept it as *one of those things*.

Without this examination we remain a *Victim to Circumstance*. We remain frightened about what will happen next. We start to shrink, we try to safeguard our *known* world and try to control what little we can. Our worlds then become minutely small; *that postage stamp world*, as we consciously or unconsciously struggle to safeguard and defend our castle against unknown invaders.

With awareness we are supported with weapons assembled from a completely different armoury, and we are in the position, a conscious position, to blend all of life's learning's and occurrences with our own experiences, understanding and examination. In this way, we are able to determine *Our Fundamental Truth*.

Once your house has been stripped bare of all its furniture and decorations, once you have removed the poor-quality contents that have accumulated within, the *Reformation* can begin.

You can reconstruct it in a way that is completely in accord with your own taste, your own flavour and your individuality. The house becomes filled only with content that *feel right to you*. You become perpetually open to further understanding, perspectives and alternative vistas of opportunity; though now you will only add this content to your property if it is in accord with your personal truth.

I do not agree with my three mentors on many of the points that they have shared with me; but now I know that that's alright. I don't have to. I am me, they are they and you are you.

Only through having the *Mastery of Self* can you be open to the *Whole* world. Only when you are complete within can you allow yourself to experience all of the external treasures this world can bring. When the house inside is beautifully created you want to share what's inside with anyone who passes your door.

Only you will know how far you are prepared to go. There will be many times of test and reflection. There will be times of massive change, times of despair. There will be times when it feels everything is stood still, *nothing* moving, *nothing* tangible to hold onto. However, *nothing* implies the tangible, the visual. *No-thing* is encased in our logic. We seek tangible proof that there is *some-thing*; there is evidence, there is visible proof.

 There will be many times on this voyage where there will be *nothing tangible* to place on the table. You will be sailing towards a horizon where you hope land is to be found, though no land is anywhere in sight. At these times one phrase needs to become of paramount reference within your being. One phrase needs to run throughout the seaside stick of rock you have purchased to give you some sugar whilst you *Resurrect & RECLAIM the True You*. That phrase is **Trust Nature & Your Being.**

Society says put your *trust* in us and we will show you the way. Society says *this* is how you need to live your life, *this* is how to be successful; *this* is how to live a life of magic. But how can *society* know?

Only you can know what is truly right for you. Once all of those layers have been removed and cleansed, you reach the stage where your core desires, your essential purposes and what you are destined to fulfil in this lifetime are revealed. Now you have *trust*; but this *trust* is emanating from your insides, not from outside forces.

This internal *trust* to follow your core desires, irrespective of outside influence, pressure or dictate, is leadership towards an enlightened, authentic life. This centre of *self-reliance, self-esteem* and *self-trust* is the pinnacle of *self-Resurrection*. When you have sufficient *trust* to act only in accordance to your inner sanctum of *self-trust*, will you know how it feels to be authentic to your intrinsic being.

Only then will you *know* how it feels for each word that flows over your lips to be in accord with your individual nature. To live in this way reveals the discipline of: *Self Trust, Openness to Opportunity with Total Responsibility.*

You attend the cinema. Very soon after the film starts you notice that you are not enjoying what you are watching. It is not stimulating you. You start to fidget, your mind wonders, your feelings are not encouraging you to watch this film any further. Your insides are uneasy; you no longer wish to be there. You stand up and leave after 30 minutes.

You are not trying to influence others; you are not trying to make a scene or trying to make yourself stand out and demonstrate a power. You simply are responding to the fact that you are not enjoying the experience. You have decided that your time is so valuable that you want to do something else that will give you joy.

The mind says 'you fool, you have paid for this film; you should give it more time, perhaps it will get better. What will other people say if you leave?' But you just *know, and you are prepared to listen to your inner voice.* Now that you are in true contact with your feelings you do not care what others think. You are not insensitive or disrespectful to others; it's just that now you are prepared to take full responsibility to do what is right for you in accordance with your *inner truth* and *your intuition*. If others wish to judge, then that's OK, that is their concern not yours. You are free to choose your experience in any given situation.

This level of freedom may appear selfish. You head may scream, 'what about the others'? I would say the following; this journey is selfish, it has to be. It is selfish in so far that it is for you to *re-find your truth*. It is selfish as the focus must be placed upon you rather than others for a period of time. Yet can you also see that this selfishness becomes selflessness, as you become the person who you were always meant to be? Can you see that only when you are complete within can you then share the whole beauty of what's inside?

At this stage you become free. Free from your past, free from conditioning, free from the constrictions of society. You are gloriously free for your future to unfold, and free to follow what is correct for you and those around you. You are free to experience life unburdened, unencumbered, unrestrained and unrestricted.

It's strange then that I could write "*I had known my purpose to that point had been to find myself. A rather naff, overly used definition, though the only one that fits with what I was searching for. So here I was, I had found me, and my reward was? 'Come on now life' I screamed, 'I have done all of these things, I have taken so many actions, now open up those doors! Reveal to me what I am supposed to see from the top of this mountain*".

When we *arrive* we often do not recognise that we are *there*!

Your *now normality* is so different from the *you* of before, but your mind still ceaselessly hankers like little Oliver's speech, 'can I have some more please Sir'! You must ensure you recognised the signs of when you have arrived home, and once again smile at the determination of the reasoning mind!

You now are once again part of the whole. You are once again connected to the universal energy rather than isolated and insulated on your tiny island.

Life becomes a *flow*, though it is not a *flow* created by you. It is a *flow* which comes from following natures' guidance. Your openness to life enables you to take every opportunity that presents itself giving your life perpetual freshness, intensity and excitement every hour of every day.

Nature asks you but one thing. It asks that you continually *take full responsibility* to *respond* to its presents, gifts and guidance, in a way that is completely in accord with your *own truth*. The *Mastery of Self* is now your possession, and furthermore; no one can ever take it away from you, unless you let them!!

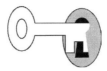

Master Keys to Resurrect & RECLAIM The True You

Realisations	The Wall of Self Esteem
	The Wall of Denial
	Total Responsibility
Experiences	Our Mind knows only what it knows!
	Review, Refresh an& Befriend non-Helpful Content of the Mind
	Trust Your Self
Choose	Conscious Choice
	Fundamental Elements of Instinct, Intuition and Trust
	Choose an& Alter Your Course According to Your Heart
Limiting Beliefs	The Mind Remembers Everything As A Fact
	Total Recall an& Completion
	Accept Your Past As Fact
	The Third Person
	Detach, View, Learn, Discard, and Smile
	Traps of Blame, an& Time and Circumstance
	What's Easy is Right
Actions and Impacts	Action Question
	Destructive Foundational Rocks
	Art of Transcendency 'If Only'!
	Power to Convert
	Lastingly Feels Right
Mastery of Self	Trust Nature and Your Being Self-Trust
	Openness to Opportunity with Total Responsibility

Printed in Great Britain
by Amazon

35664629R00082